PERMANENT TRANSIENCE

Bendle

Bendle

For Yarrow
& for Nag and Igor and Giblet

In memory of Else and Protag

2nd Edition

First published in digital form 2015

First paper edition 1st Jan 2018

Cover photo by Snotcher

MUDDYCROW PUBLISHING

CONTENTS

Preface 5
PART ONE 7
Cryptic 8
Chain of Dots 10
Potter 14
Queen's Hotel 15
SIC 18
Kings Cross 21
Vote Conservative 24
Porky Prime Cut 26
Giblet 29
Snotcher 32
Matlock 35
Shopping 40
LMC 42
Peel 45
Eyebrow 49
The Sound of Music 52
Travel 54
Friends and Allies 56
Alison 62
Tufnell Park Mob 64
Crass 66
Style and Influences 68
Bad Music 70
Mushrooms 73
Hippies 77
Weird Noise 81

Christmas	86
49 Americans	88
Orbit of Scritti	90
Street Level Studio	92
Mark	97
Detailed Twang	99
Double Drums	102
Street Level Again	105
Improv	108
Twang	112
Romance	116
More Gigs	117
Beat the Tory Blues	120
Jazz Punk Bonanza	123
On Tour in Europe	126
The End	134
PART TWO	136
Watford	137
Squeekybop Jugband	147
Dogs	159
Afterword	162
Endnotes	163

Preface

In writing my version of the story of The Door And The Window I have focussed mainly upon the first phase of the band's existence, because it reflects a unique point in the history of (un)popular music. For a brief couple of years after the commercialisation (and subsequent redundancy) of punk music it was possible to produce and market all sorts of weird music and noise. Nag and I had a keen interest in playing music and in running our own record company. Despite having no business sense and no musical competence we managed to make and sell records – to an underground audience that was small, but which was widely (internationally) scattered. I felt myself to be one of a tangible community of musicians supporting each other with equipment and information, and of a wider community of people putting out their own music on small labels. Rather than a sense of competition, or envy at other bands having bigger audiences or sales there was a spirit of one of the gang doing well. We were constantly bemused at our own success and that people kept offering us work and exposure.

I have written more briefly of later incarnations of the band, because our gigs got less frequent, and to put them fully into context would have meant a book several times longer. The importance of the later versions of TDATW for me is that we continued to demonstrate the Permanent Transience that we had initially claimed as our modus operandi.

I have tried to be as true as I can be to my experience of the story of The Door and The Window, although this has been written may years after the events. I have used old diaries as sources of information, but realise that I didn't bother to record many things that were familiar enough to be taken for granted at the time. I have chosen to leave out details that I cannot date or corroborate and have aimed to avoid retrospective analysis in an attempt at recapturing some of the spirit of that time.

Thanks to everyone mentioned in the story, and apologies to those missed out. Please get in touch if you think I've got any parts of the story wrong!

PERMANENT
TRANSIENCE
Side
one
THE
DOOR
AND THE
WINDOW
NB
2
100 50 0

PART ONE

Cryptic

November and it was cold. I stood eyeing the other punters with a bit of card in my hand with the single word *Igor* written on it. He had told me he'd be wearing a plastic ladder, whatever that meant. Nag would be with him, though I didn't know if he would be wearing a ladder or not. A scrawny man with long hair and a beard approached me – Are you looking for Igor? Yes, I said, is that you..? – no he wasn't Igor, his name was Steve but he knew the person I was looking for and would point him out to me when he got there. Steve invited me to come on into the warm, so I followed him down into the crypt below the church where there was a small stage set up for the music which I knew was the future of music happening tonight.

Nag and Igor arrived soon after, with a third young bloke called Psi. Their coat pockets were full of tins of beer and they passed one to me. The place was smoky and crowded and the stage hard to see because of pillars supporting the church above us. Igor's ladder was tiny - a sort of cocktail stick decoration pinned to his dead man's overcoat. He was tall, also long-haired and had a little beard divided into two forks. He was friendly and reassuring, relaxed. Nag was speeding, though I didn't recognise this yet, jabbering away and pointing out musicians and journalists from the NME and Sounds. He'd talk with Igor and Steve and me then whiz off to cajole or insult someone. I was impressed – not only did he recognise all these famous people but he felt able to be rude to them.

The music was a blur and I was too excited to retain any critical perspective – here were Robert Rental & The Normal, Metabolist, Cabaret Voltaire and Throbbing Gristle all squashed into one little subterranean room making the sound of tomorrow. Nag would vanish and then reappear. I lost touch with Steve, but met Dennis Burns from another of my hero bands – Alternative TV. Dennis looked like Mr Normal Suburban Man with a boring jumper and he was holding his bicycle lights and pump. I liked his lack of pretension and I liked that he had come on a bike. I talked to him between sets and then craned my head to try to get a view of the stage. Genesis P Orridge came on and made a little joke about what was just finishing on telly, that this was a family show. I'd expected to be blasted by a wall of noise by Throbbing Gristle, I'd not expected the sense of humour. They beamed a spotlight onto the audience, so perhaps they could see us, but we were just dazzled. I loved them.

I'd arranged by letter to stay with Nag and Igor. They lived in Muswell Hill, though I didn't know where that was. I knew them by way of my membership of the Society for the Introduction of Confusion. Psi came back from Paddington with us in a taxi – it was late and the buses were stopping. I anxiously watched the fare ticking its way upwards on the meter of the black cab, unsure if I could afford my share. Perhaps the others watched it too – when it pulled up, we scratched together enough to pay the fare. The taxi driver left us with an insult about our minuscule tip.

Just outside where they lived, there was a very deep hole in the road – perhaps 20 feet and a long ladder which tapered towards the top was leaning against the corrugated iron that surrounded the hole. Psi insisted that we extract the ladder and invert it – surely we should take every opportunity to introduce a little confusion? I helped him, but was wary of getting mud all over my army greatcoat. Psi didn't seem to care. We talked for a while in Igor and Nag's flat, then Psi and I tried to sleep as best we could on a settee and cushions.

The next day Igor and Nag were doing surprisingly mundane Sunday things like going to see their respective parents. I don't know what Psi was doing. We promised to keep in touch and I set off via a misunderstood public transport system to St Pancras station and thence back to Matlock.

Chain of Dots

January 1979 and I was heading back to London. Toerag, whose family lived in Shepherd's Bush was travelling with me. We'd found an advert and responded to a guy who made a regular trip from Matlock to London. For a small share of the cost of his petrol we could get to the capital for much less than the price of the train. Snow was falling heavily and in places the M1 was reduced to one lane in each direction. The car radio informed us that it was unwise to travel. Slowly we made our way south. Once in London the snow was less deep. We made our way to Toerag's house and said hello to his Dad, and then vanished to the pub to meet his friends. We returned after closing time and Toerag started to fry up a meal. In my own parents' home I'd have crept about trying not to wake them, but Toerag was drunkenly crashing about frying bread and sausages and eggs and bacon. London Irish, Toerag had a great down to earth sense of humour. He was studying books that I had never heard of – but which I would soon be reading myself – and describing them to me: This book, right, Waiting for Godot, it's about these two geezers, right, and they're waiting for this other geezer, right – and he never fucking comes!

We ate our late supper and we both squeezed into Toerag's bed to sleep. We had breakfast together in the morning and I said I'd see him the following night for the return journey. Then I made my way across London by tube to Turnpike Lane to meet Nag and Igor again. They had moved from their flat in Muswell Hill to a maisonette in Hornsey. They met me and also a young guy called Garry, who had travelled down from Grimsby.

I'd been in touch with Garry via a newsletter issued by Throbbing Gristle. He wanted to form a band - sound, he said, = noise and noise = sound. Well I was willing to go along with that, and so were several others, including, when I put them in touch with him, Nag and Igor. The people that had contacted Garry lived all over the country - one near York, one in Brighton, one in Norfolk, me in Matlock and Igor and Nag in London. Garry had a name that expressed an idea. The band was called Chain of Dots and we made music (initially) by Jamming By Post. Each of us had two cassette recorders. One of us would initiate some noise – record it and send it on to a second person. They would play along with the tape and record it onto a second cassette, then post it to another participant. Anyone could start a piece of music or noise. And Garry had a plan about performing live. If two or more members could get together to perform then they could use the band name. We liked the possibility of there being two gigs by the same band, on the same night but in different places. I had met Garry once, when I had travelled to Grimsby, which is where I had bought my second hand Jedson electric guitar. He had a drum kit and we had recorded a din together. Now he was in London to hear Throbbing Gristle play their next gig at a place called the Centro Iberico on Sunday lunchtime.

Pretty soon after we got together Garry, Nag and Igor were encouraging me to stay longer than just one night. I felt that I should get back to college, they felt that I should hang around and we could start being a band. Garry had the week off of work and we had our first "official" planned rehearsals the following weekend with a guy called Colin near York. I argued against them but my urge to go back to lectures seemed a bit pathetic really. I knew when I left school that what I wanted to do was make music. The fact that I couldn't really play anything seemed like an advantage to me, but didn't impress my parents nor schoolteachers who had urged me into teacher training college. I was just into my second term and it was horrible. I told my new friends that I would stay in London. I felt guilty, but decided to phone the college on Monday and say that the snow made it impossible to get back.

Sunday saw us gathered with a crowd of the faithful in what turned out to be an old school building in West London. In place of a support act TG were showing their short black and white film *After Cease to Exist* - grainy, dark, narratively and morally obscure. Was that a castration? I didn't like it, but that was probably the point – after all this was a band that used the worst of humanity's acts as a starting point for their art and part of what they did was to present a challenge. I didn't quite understand the challenge, but understood that I had to question what they were doing, not just swallow it all. Noise-wise the gig was great. Why did I love this harsh "Industrial" noise? Because they were honest and totally uncompromising, and because if they could do it, I could do it. Musically they had wiped the slate clean, much more so than punk. Now anything was possible.

At the end of the gig we got to say hello to the band, who were very friendly. Cosey and Genesis remembered my and Garry's names from our correspondence with them and we chatted to them as they packed away their instruments and gadgets. I had begun writing to them initially by accident, ordering a single from Industrial Records by post, and being surprised by a personal note in with the record. I wrote back and subsequently received copies their newsletter, *Industrial News*.

Igor was working in a record shop and was out in the daytime. Nag had recently packed in his job at another branch of the same store and was free to spend time making noise together with Garry and I. The maisonette had a slightly grotty basement living room space where there were two 6 foot mattresses from a fold down settee on which Garry and I slept, covered with a pile of coats. In the day we sat on these pottering with Nag's Wasp synthesiser. This was a small black and yellow plastic contraption, with lots of confusing knobs and a touch sensitive keyboard – the first budget synth. Also in the front room there was an old banjo and Igor's slightly knackered violin. Igor's keyboard and amp were also in there. Igor could actually play in a conventional sense and was the keyboard player in a new wave group called Blue Screaming.

We got the idea that we should play a gig. There was a band called Dead Fingers Talk playing at the Nashville Rooms on the Tuesday night. I'd heard the name but not heard their music. Nag and Igor said that they were quite a straight forward rock band but that they had an amazing singer who was worth witnessing. We set off on the tube, each with a can of Special Brew, with the idea of being their support band. We had Nag's Wasp, the banjo and the violin. We also had a spoon and Garry had a packet of space dust. What sounded like some sort of novel drug was actually just a gimmicky sweet powder that made a popping noise in your mouth. I was scared stiff, but if we were going to be a band then we had to make a start. A down and out on the tube train asked for a swig of our beer. We gave him some and asked if he wanted to join our band. He declined. We turned up at the venue – a big London pub – and said hello, and that we were the support band. No one asked our band's name, they just let us in, saying that when Dead Fingers Talk had finished their sound check we would have time for a short one ourselves. We were dreading the arrival of the real support act but they didn't show up. We watched Dead Fingers Talk sorting out their sound. Mick Ronson who had played with David Bowie had just produced their recent album and was hanging around keeping an eye on things.

When it came to our turn we said that we just needed three microphones and somewhere to plug in the Wasp, and by the time we'd sorted that the audience was coming in. We had no idea what we were going to do, but were aware that there were four of us and that we had only three instruments. We agreed to swap instruments as we went along. Being the person singing or speaking or whatever seemed the most daunting role, and Igor having the most experience of being on a stage said he'd start off with no instrument to hide behind.

We took the stage when directed to do so, noodling with our respective instruments,

Igor standing at the mic. He said - this first tune is called debate: if you have anything you want to discuss then you can come up here and put your ideas forward. The audience seemed bemused and wary, standing in an arc around the stage while we plinked and plonked – I was sat on a chair and had the banjo flat on my lap plucking the strings with the spoon. At times our improvisation got slightly rhythmic, but never quite became a song. At one point we all found ourselves half singing half shouting "Dolores" over and over. I had no idea what it meant, and it was only later that I found that it was the name of a friend of Nag and Igor's. Garry made space dust noise into the microphone and hit the mic stand with the spoon. We managed about 20 minutes before the bouncers physically pulled us from the stage. We had recorded the gig on Igor's cassette recorder and after being removed from the stage wandered amongst the audience soliciting their reactions to our noise. A few liked it, most disliked it and some said it was so bad that they were going to form their own band because they could do better. This seemed to be a good reaction to us, so we rated the event a success. The place was packed, we had had a good audience for our first performance.

When Dead Fingers Talk came on we squeezed our way to the front, where I found myself next to Mick Ronson. I thought I was getting to mix with famous people but when I started dancing Mr Ronson objected and hit me in the face. Still, it was a claim to fame, getting punched by David Bowie's guitarist.

The next day we thought that perhaps we could get a gig somewhere else. Essential Logic were playing at the Moonlight Club. We took a different approach this time and phoned the venue – we were a new band, only in London for a few days, could we do a short slot at the beginning of the evening – we didn't want payment? They said yes, just turn up later. We were on a roll. But some hours later, when we were at the club, the manager approached us and asked – were we the band who had played at the Nashville rooms the night before? Yes we were, we answered proudly. In that case, he said, he didn't want us playing at his venue, but as a goodwill gesture we could stay and listen to the other bands for free.

Potter

On Friday at the end of that week Nag and Garry and I caught a coach from Victoria coach station up to York for our first official Chain of Dots rehearsals. Igor had chosen not to travel north. We bought our tickets and went to get a cup of tea in the cafe, sitting down at a table for four with a middle-aged woman who was already seated. We had just sat down when Genesis P Orridge wandered into the cafe, about to catch a coach himself. We said hello, and he responded by asking in a loud voice if I still had a bad case of crabs. This resulted in his desired effect of prompting the woman at our table to leave, and he took her place to join us for a chat and a cup of tea. Genesis talked about the second TG album that was coming out soon, and mentioned the band's little joke. Their single *United* had sold relatively well and was very accessible compared to their other noise. They had included it on the new album which they were hoping to shrink wrap, with a sticker on the front saying "including the hit single". But for the album they had sped up the original tape of the recording so that *United* was only 16 seconds long! He wished us luck with our Chain of Dots adventure and we took it as a good omen that our paths had crossed.

Colin Potter met us from the coach station and drove us to his house in a small village where we stayed for the weekend. He was older than us and was married. He also had lots more instruments and amplifiers. He had hired a local church hall for a day and half of our noise making. I loved it – hours of chugging rhythms, inept krautrock dirge, all recorded onto cassette. Garry, Nag and I were in heaven, though Colin hoped that we might have a little more musical ability or perhaps just that we might be able to listen to each other more sensitively. He wrote us a carefully worded letter in the following week saying that he'd not gotten what he wanted from the experience, that we needed a little more discipline, and that he was parting from Chain of Dots. He was generous with us, and in the evenings introduced us to experimental music from his collection. All I'd ever heard was variants of pop and rock music, with Lou Reed's Metal Machine Music and Throbbing Gristle marking an extreme end of this range. Colin played us his friend Trevor Wishart's rather scary *Red Bird* – a collage of spoken word where human screams morph into those of seagulls and the sounds of creaking doors.

Queen's Hotel

I had been writing to Nag and Igor for over a year, and our communication had gotten more frequent once we had discovered that our musical interests overlapped. Whilst still at school I'd sent them a tape of a musical collage I had made and once they joined the ranks of Chain of Dots we sent music back and forth. We also sent each other all sorts of junk, and although we first posted our correspondence in envelopes, soon we were sending letters in plastic bottles and bin liner bags, or writing postcards on bits of plastic. Igor smoked, and I had discovered a cigarette vending machine at the college that could be cheated – put fifty pence in, pull out the drawer very slowly and out would come both the fifty pence piece, and a packet of ten cigarettes with three pence change. So I would steal from the machine to send cigarettes to Igor as well.

Nag sent me postcards urging me to leave my silly college course and to move down to London. There was a small third bedroom in the maisonette in Hornsey which could be mine if I wanted to move in with them. I prevaricated for a while and then made the decision that I would. I had made some friends among the locals but had very few people I felt I could trust among my fellow students, who mostly saw me as a weirdo. There was a small village atmosphere around the college and weirdos needed to be bashed into line. I'd had enough of being (literally) bashed.

Garry had arranged our next gig at the Queen's Hotel in Cleethorpes. The gig coincided with my college Easter holiday. I travelled down from Matlock to Swindon to see my parents and to make them aware of my decision, that I wouldn't be returning to Matlock after the holiday. They were surprised and upset, but surprisingly supportive. Bang went their hopes that I "would do better than them". I said I'd move in with Nag and Igor and get a job.

I got a train to London and stayed with Nag and Igor for a few days before the gig. We would be better prepared this time – I'd have my guitar and one of my reel to reel tape recorders. Nag and I wandered Hornsey with a cassette recorder recording our conversations with the populace. Our favourite interviewee was an old guy who said – Do what? I can't be buggered about with that, I'm doing this! We looped his voice a dozen times over onto the reel to reel tape for the gig.

Both Nag and I, though, had some misgivings about Garry – he seemed a bit too keen on the grim imagery that Throbbing Gristle put out, and at our last meeting had kept asking – do you think I'm evil? He was disappointed when we answered no. We discussed our doubts with Igor, who was not on board for the Grimsby gig. He said – why don't you forget about Garry, form a duo and call yourselves...uh – looking around - The Door And The Window? We liked the idea and said we'd think on it.

The idea took hold quickly: on the way to Grimsby Nag and I stopped to visit the office of Company Records in Lincoln. Company was one of a number of small independent labels that had sprung up in the wake of punk and was run by Chris Hall from his home. We had phoned and asked if we could call in. When we arrived we explained that we were a new industrial noise group called The Door And The Window, and that we were hoping for a recording contract. Given we had nothing to play him, nor any evidence of what we were up to Chris was understandably cautious but he said to keep in touch and that we should send him recordings to listen to. Then he played us his latest releases and enthused about one of these by a guy called Wavis O'Shave who seemed to be bonkers and, to the sound of jarring angular guitar, sang songs about fig roll biscuits and shoes.

In Grimsby we met Richard from Norwich for the first time and Garry had enrolled a couple of others and between us we carried guitars and drums and amplifiers and a rubbish TV and my reel to reel via public transport to Cleethorpes. We wanted to run the telly silently all the way through the performance to accompany the recordings that Nag and I had made. A (proper) local band played first and then we came on. We had more volume than at the Nashville Rooms. We maybe were musically incompetent and clueless as to how the evening would progress, but we made up for it with raw enthusiasm. The manager of the Queens hotel, however, took a strong dislike to the feedback and shouting spilling into his bar from the room above. He ran upstairs and turned off the main power supply. For a second there was silence then someone in the audience asked why the manager had done that and someone else threw a chair at him. Suddenly the room erupted in a Cleethorpes version of a cowboy bar room brawl. Nag and I backed off and ducked behind the PA speakers and waited for things to cool down.

Afterwards we struggled back towards Garry's place without any transport. Passing the railway station and realising that it seemed to have finished business for the day

Richard suggested we get on a train and sleep the night there. We found a train and the gang of us settled down in some chairs. After a few minutes Richard announced that perhaps he'd take us for a ride – it can't be too hard to drive a train! He got stopped whilst trying to get into the cab and we were all evicted from the station by the Transport Police. In the street outside the station some drunken folk in a transit van skidded to a halt and asked if we were the band that had been playing at the Queen's Hotel? I was unsure how to answer – if we admitted it, might we get beaten up? Garry, however, proudly said that yes, we were. Great they said, get in, we'll take you to a party. So we all piled into the back of the van with our gear and were taken to our first post gig party.

SIC

I moved into the tiny bedroom in Ferrestone Road, paying a rent of £6 per week. The fold down settee made a double bed which took up three quarters of the room. Igor had a medium sized bedroom and Nag had the biggest – but it had a settee in it and we used his room as a living room in the daytime. The three bedrooms were on the upper floor. Downstairs was the room where Garry and I had slept in January – now designated as a rehearsal room. In case people were unclear about the function of the room it had a sign leaning against the wall saying Rehearsal Rehearsals – Nag and Igor had nicked it from the Clash from outside their place in Chalk Farm[i]. Also downstairs we had a large kitchen with built in units, a gas cooker, a sink and a fridge. There were no table or chairs. There was an off-shot bathroom and tacked on the end of that a small toilet. For heating there was a gas fire in the rehearsal room and there was one electric convection heater that we shared between us. We had a tiny front garden, but a door in the kitchen led to a larger back one which looked out on a small old graveyard, and the tower of the former St Mary's church. At the end of the garden were several huge black Italian poplar trees.

Because my room was so tiny, I was inspired from the outset to keep it immaculately tidy. I kept my clothes in a suitcase under my bed and in a little bedside cabinet. I carefully made my bed each morning and when I could bought flowers to put in a cheap vase on the cabinet. My parents had bought me a quilt and cover – which was a new thing for both them and for me. I'd slept under sheet and blankets up until this point. My parents were concerned by my needing bedding for a double bed rather than a single, but I pointed out that that was what the room came with.

London in 1979 was a mess. It was the Winter of Discontent when anyone and everyone was going on strike. For some weeks earlier in the year there had been no refuse collections and there were still piles of rubbish outside of shops and houses, sometimes with attendant rats. The MP Airey Neave had just been killed by the Irish National Liberation Army with a car bomb as he left the House of Commons.

The nearby shops in Turnpike Lane and Tottenham Lane were mostly Cypriot and

PERMANENT TRANSIENCE

Asian and were full of new foods for me to try. We bought flat Cypriot loaves of bread, and Nag astonished me by frying some carrots – I began to discover that there was more to veg than just boiling them. He introduced me to condensed coconut and tamarind which we added to our vegetable curries.

In my first week in London I found fifty pounds rolled up on the ground. My intention was to hand it in to the police, but I used some of it because I was broke. Subsequently I decided to spend the rest of it on an amplifier for my guitar. Previously I had been using a reel to reel recorder as a small amp. Suddenly I now had a big second-hand valve bass amp and a four foot high speaker cabinet. Nag bought an amp and speaker combo from the same place just up the road in Hornsey and one at a time we carried them home. The bloke who sold them to us said that the equipment had previously belonged to the old sixties (and seventies revival) rock and roll band The Pirates.

I signed on as unemployed. Igor had packed in his job as well, so all three of us were on the dole. Registering as unemployed involved appointments at the Job Centre in Wood Green, the issuing of a UB40 form at an office in Palmers Green and then a visit to the DHSS in an office tower block in Archway. Subsequently I would have to sign on for my Supplementary Benefit fortnightly in Palmers Green.

Nag and I had a plan: we were a band and we would do what bands did – we would record records and play gigs. Igor's band Blue Screaming had had one single released on the tiny Albatross Records label. He explained to us that we didn't need to get signed up – we could put out a record ourselves. We knew of a number of bands who had done this including a band called Scritti Politti with whom Igor was friends, and with whom he could discuss the practicalities. Nag and I came up with a name: NB Records, and declared ourselves in business. We opened a bank account and I designed some headed paper.

But we weren't instantly playing lots of music. After having to fight against constraints for most of my life I felt a little lost in my new freedom. Nag snapped at me and told me to stop following him around – it didn't need two of us to go and buy a petty cash book. My new flat mates presented me with a ring binder folder full of letters and addresses. They informed me that I was now the administrator of The Society for the Introduction of Confusion. I was duly confused. Igor had started SIC 18 months previously. With no real aim in mind he had advertised free membership in the small ads in a music paper, and that was how I had joined. Nag had been out of the country but had helped him with running SIC when he had returned from a kibbutz in Israel. Every now and again they had issued a newsletter with ideas to inspire chaos inducing activity. In one edition there had been a drawing of a UFO and a map of the UK with a line drawn running from North to South. Next to the line were marked times that the supposed UFO would be visible at that location on a stated date. We could then all report reasonably similar sightings to local papers and radio stations – and let the media link their reports together. I had designed the logo for SIC, a six pointed arrow.

My main chaotic activity had been sending weird collections of photocopied material to addresses picked from the phone directory. On the back of the envelope would be a return address also picked at random from the phone directory. Now, seemingly I had control of the whole shebang. I felt uninspired and worried about how I would be judged if I had no ideas.

Meanwhile we had political duties to attend to. Prompted by a vote of no confidence in Jim Callaghan's Labour administration, there was a general election due in less than a month. Capitalising on the general dissatisfaction with the Labour government, The National Front were trying to drum up support and to get some votes. Mostly they seemed to attract skinhead thugs, but they were fielding over 300 candidates in the forthcoming election. They were having a public meeting in Islington Town Hall and we would be amongst those trying to deny them a platform.

The police were out in force, supposedly a neutral line between the NF supporters and the Anti-Nazi League protesters, but it seemed to us that they were being more protective of the NF meeting than of those aiming to stop it. Foolishly we decided to infiltrate the meeting. Igor had his portable cassette recorder with him and we told the police that we were journalists. Somehow we got through the police line and into the queue of people going into the building. All the others in the queue seemed to be either thugs in suits or thugs in jeans and braces. The guys on the door stopped us. Press, we said. Igor waved his cassette recorder and they let him in – You two can fuck off.

Nag and I joined the protesters chanting outside. There were a few minor skirmishes but I was relieved that the event did not turn violent. Three days later a similar demonstration on the far side of London outside Southall Town Hall would lead to Clarence Baker, from the reggae band Misty in Roots, being in a coma for months and to the death of schoolteacher Blair Peach. The hated police unit the SPG – the Special Patrol Group - were blamed for his death. Back in Islington we fretted about how Igor was getting on in the town hall. We didn't see him again until later that evening back at home. He had discreetly taped part of the meeting but lost his nerve and decided to leave. As he made his way to the door he was heckled: Sloppy bollocks.

Kings Cross

The next night Nag and I went to see an anarchist band called Charge at a small venue in Camden town. I made the most of my young looks – realising that although I was 18 I could pass for 15 and get half fares on the buses. Nag was three years older than me but would also try to get half fares. The admission fee was small, so we could afford a tin or two of beer and enjoyed pogoing around to the thrashy pop music.

We caught the 29 bus back to Turnpike lane and wandered up the road, looking for useful trash outside the shops. We found a blue formica topped kitchen table near a cafe and carried it the length of Turnpike Lane. Along the way we picked up a crate of rotten tomatoes from amongst the heaps of rubbish that were still littering the streets. Stopping for a rest where the railway line crosses the road (and the New River runs underneath) we started pelting a billboard advert for jeans with the tomatoes whilst chanting – the National Front is a Nazi front, smash the National Front! Totally absorbed in our activity we failed to spot the police car until it had pulled up next to us:
And what are you two doing?
We're throwing tomatoes at an advert.
And where did you get the tomatoes?
From a pile of rubbish back there.
And the table?
The same.
They were about to take down our details when they got a call through on their radio that there was some kind of emergency: Wait right there, they said and zoomed off. Nag and I stood bemused for a moment then picked up the table and ran the rest of the way home. Now our kitchen had a table.

Psi came to visit and invited me to go back to his place in King's Cross. Whilst waiting on the overground station in Hornsey he spotted a timer switch in the waiting room. It was a large button which once depressed would turn on a heater. Slowly it would return to its original setting and turn the heater off. Psi said that he could make use of it, and opened the small toolbox that he had with him and removed it from the wall. He neatly covered the ends of the exposed wires with insulating tape and stuck a little note to the wall: Danger, live wires. Then he packed his new toy and his tools away and we boarded a train.

Psi was living in a short life housing association property just behind Kings Cross station, with two other blokes called Simon (Pearce) and Godfrey. All three of them were members of Blue Screaming. He showed me a shortcut out of the back of the station through a small goods yard. Near the station exit there were crates of empty bottles from the station bar. Spotting that a bottle had some wine left in it, Psi liberated it from the crate and began to guzzle it. As he held it out to offer me the dregs we were stopped by a Transport Police officer who demanded that we follow him to his office in a porta-cabin across the way. Psi seemed nonchalant, but I was scared. First I'd been stopped with Nag, now I was being picked up by the police. The officer sat us down and took our details and got us to empty our pockets. When this failed to produce anything incriminating he asked Psi to open his tool box. Slowly he took out one object at a time. He sniffed at a piece of tinfoil and said – this has been used to wrap some cannabis, I think. I guessed that he was bluffing and that he was toying with us, but what he said was possibly true. Then, considering the bits and pieces of electrical gear asked what was Psi's excuse for carrying it around. Psi explained that he was a musician and that he mended amplifiers and was building a PA. Yes? said the policeman, I think what we have here is bomb making equipment. I thought: surely we'd need Irish accents to go with that accusation? You realise that I can keep you here for 24 hours without charging you? I was getting increasingly nervous and this sadist was enjoying it, but after an hour or so he let us go.

We walked slowly away from the porta-cabin police station and around the corner to Stanley Buildings, and up to Psi's third floor flat, where he decided we needed something to help us relax after enduring the police interrogation. He decided it was time to harvest and smoke a few leaves from Simon's cannabis plant. Whenever I had smoked cannabis before I had had to endure the negative effects of smoking tobacco with it, but Psi introduced me to the idea of rolling it with dried mint, which was much more pleasurable. And then he took me up to the flat roof of the building from where we were able to look out at views of Kings Cross and Saint Pancras Stations on one side and at huge gas storage tanks on the other.

Back down to his flat. To get to the toilet you had to go through Cy's bedroom. This had all of the walls and the ceiling covered in egg trays which had been spray painted black. The window was covered over too. The light switch had a little glowing light on it so that it could be located in the dark. The egg boxes had been put there as an attempt to soundproof the room, which at one time they had thought might be used as a practice space. Cy's bed was elevated up on a platform, and below it there was a desk with all of his electrical gear including an impressive looking oscilloscope.

Vote Conservative

Nag and I had been busking on the underground at Finsbury Park. It was our first encounter with the bureaucracy of buskers – having to book a pitch and having to play in the right place. We'd just turned up and started plinking away, untunefully, with Nags Wasp which had a little inbuilt speaker and a borrowed crap acoustic guitar. We'd been threatened by other buskers and earned derisory comments from the public. We had earned 21p. Wandering back home through the side streets of Hornsey we saw a house with a sign in the window: Conservative Party Campaign Headquarters. Without needing to discuss our action we walked up to the door and asked if we could help with the campaign. Nag in his overcoat and me in my army greatcoat didn't look too scruffy, yes we could help, and if we were free at the moment we could help with their envelope stuffing session. The Post Office had agreed to deliver one leaflet to each household for each major political party, and inside the house a little group of middle aged ladies and one or two older men were folding leaflets and putting them into envelopes.

Nag and I eagerly accepted piles of A4 propaganda. Diligently we folded our pieces of paper in three and tucked them into the envelopes. Methodically we placed nine or ten leaflets in roughly every tenth envelope and left the others empty. Our completed piles were of comparable size and weight to those that had been done correctly. We were praised for our youthful speed and enthusiasm, and we said we'd be delighted to come back and help again. And did they have any posters that we could display on behalf of Hugh Rossi – the current Hornsey MP – so that we might help him to retain his seat?

We took the posters home and carefully cut them up and collaged new ones. Some time ago Nag and Igor had produced a fanzine called The New Wave Magazine with a guy called Ade. Ade worked as a designer and printer and had furnished us with a good supply of Letraset lettering in various sizes and fonts, and we used these to design our own versions of Conservative Party posters, complete with official logos and addresses and phone numbers. Mostly our creations were blatantly racist, because we thought this might be the easiest way to offend a good proportion of the locals, and thus lose Mr Rossi some votes. We photocopied our posters at the HCVS – the Haringey Council for Voluntary Service – the cheapest place to get photocopying and Gestener printing done. Then we fly-posted them onto places like church noticeboards.

The local Tory party offices were just up the road from where we lived, on Tottenham lane, and we took to spitting on the window at night (as did many other locals) on the way back from the Railway pub in Crouch End.

Porky Prime Cut

Nag and I did some planning towards our goals of making records and playing live. Igor's band had a couple of gigs coming up, and we were invited to play at the second of these at a place called Mayhem – a converted British Rail warehouse used as a studio by (minor pop star) Toyah Wilcox. There would be just the two of us and a tape recorder, but maybe that would change at different performances. Without knowing anything about jazz, I suggested that we behave like jazz performers. It seemed to me that pop and rock musicians got overly attached to the identities of the bands they were in, but that jazz musicians seemed to move between different ensembles. Nag came up with a name for my aspiration: Permanent Transience. We had no idea whom we might invite to play with us, nor when, but we liked the idea.

Having decided to make a single, we decided to design the cover. We went out to take photos, of partially demolished buildings, of ourselves, and of our recording gear – guitar, Wasp and reel to reel on a chair in the garden. We knew that singles would be delivered in plain white sleeves so we began to design a 14 X 7 inch wrapper to fold around them. And then we thought that maybe we should record some music.

With a view to recording there we booked time at the Alan Gordon rehearsal studios in Leyton and turned up with the Wasp, my guitar, a borrowed fuzzbox and a cassette recorder. And some beer. It was my first visit to a rehearsal room, and I was struck by the squalor. The place was equipped with several amplifiers and microphones. There was a carpet on the floor that seemed to be 50% composed of fag ash and the whole place stank of stale spilled beer. On the plus side it seemed to be a place where we could get away with anything. We thrashed and bashed – there was a drum kit in the studio which we used - and we made up songs as we went along. We had several tapes and recorded everything, including the intervention of the owner (Alan?) of the studio, who stuck his head round the door saying: Christ, we get lots of bands in these studios, but you're the worst band I've ever heard. We turned his words into a song and sang it drunkenly back at him. He slammed the door and left us to it. Nag, in a weird wimpy voice, accompanied with my sporadic drumming, sang a great free-flowing song about his "two end feeling" (...*and rebuff was the word for a pint of water, axe Maggie Thatcher on a horse...!*) and I made up some good words on the spot initially inspired by the names of bands (like Iron Fist Ruler) scrawled on the walls. At the end of the day we made our way home by bus and tube feeling that we had done a good day's work.

We were keen to meet as many people as possible in what we saw as the worlds of industrial and electronic music. We found that a guy called Thomas Leer (who had released a great single called *Private Plane* the previous year) lived nearby, and we made contact with Simon Leonard from a group called File Under Pop. FUP had a single out on Rough Trade, called *Heathrow*, that seemed to be cut ups of ambient and synthesised industrial noise. And recordings of an airport. Simon lived in Camden and invited us round. He was a slightly socially awkward character, especially compared to Nag who seemed to be able to chat easily with anyone, but he was welcoming and willing to share his time. We had turned up with Nag's Wasp, and we played with this and Simon's more expensive synthesisers. Leonard was technically proficient, and demonstrated how we could run chains of synths together. We recorded bits and pieces on Igor's cassette recorder.

We called round on Leer and found that he lived in a little bedsit with his girlfriend. He was also friendly and welcoming. He explained that he monitored all of his recordings through headphones, not wanting to make any noise to disturb his girlfriend or the neighbours. We drank the tea he offered us, but didn't feel that we should stay too long. We said that we would call back. Walking home through Hornsey we found a house where it seemed that someone had died or been evicted and where all the left behind furniture had been thrown out on the street. The house itself was empty. We found four usable kitchen chairs and carried two home each to use with our formica table.

A friend of Nag and Igor's came round armed with a high quality two track recorder to record us playing stuff at home for the single, but we were uninspired. We decided to issue an EP of four tunes – 3 from the rehearsal studio (including the *Wurst Band* song) and a snippet of Wasp that Nag had played through one of Simon Leonard's synths (now titled *Nostradamus*).

Nag had a few hundred pounds in his savings. I had about £5. Between us we had enough to manufacture a thousand singles.

Igor had supplied us with the details of how to proceed. The first stage was to take our edited recordings to a mastering room and get a master copy of our single cut. We ended up booking time in a cutting room with a guy called George Peckham, in a suite of studios across the road from the BBC building in Portland Place. George laughed at the incompetence of our turning up with a cassette tape instead of a professional quarter inch tape. He laughed at our music. He laughed at everything – he seemed to be a perpetually Mr Happy. He reminded me of those Chinese fat laughing Buddha statues. He cut each side of our disc and then asked if we wanted anything scratched in the run out groove – which would then appear on all copies of our disc. He explained that if we didn't mind, he would add his trademark: A Porky Prime Cut. Wow! All through our teens, Nag and I had been spotting that graffito cut onto our records, and now we knew where it came from. We asked him if he would put: Is that a bell? (referring to a bell-like noise on *Nostradamus*) on the A side and This is the worst record I have ever cut – Porky, on the B side. He happily complied and our session ended with more of his contagious laughter. Leaving his studio we bumped into members of the glam rock band Slade who were rehearsing down the corridor. We were bemused – we thought that they had split up years ago. We recognised their faces, but they were nameless – the drummer and the guitarist, not Noddy Holder nor Dave Hill.

Giblet

Between recording our first single and getting it cut we met Giblet. A Thursday morning and Nag and I were busking again at Finsbury Park tube station. The long subterranean corridors added a bit of alluring reverb to our din, but there was probably little else to prompt people to throw money in our hat. A boy who seemed to be about my age passed by and hesitated for a moment. He asked Nag if he had been at a couple of gigs where he might have spotted him. When Nag said that yes, he had been there, his inquisitor asked – and was it you and some other boy that were running around the venue at the Ramones gig at The Roundhouse? Yes it was. Our new friend introduced himself as Andrew. Surely you have a better name than that? Nag asked. Uh...you can call me Giblet. He asked could he join us for a while?

Giblet wrote songs, some of which were easy to learn, catchy and humorous:

> ants are crawling on the ground
> ants are deep, ants are profound
> ants will show you what to do
> ants will make your grey skies blue...

So we joined in with him rather than the other way round. I was in the habit of always carrying a notebook and pen in one of the many pockets of my green NATO military jacket, and we swapped addresses and phone numbers. Giblet lived about a mile or so up the road from us on the rise up to Muswell Hill – we agreed to meet again soon. We had even earned a few pence.

It was the third of May, and was polling day for the general election. I had cast a postal vote in Swindon for the Labour candidate, so had no civic duties for that day. We spent the afternoon loafing around in Nag's room listening to music. Our original link with each other had been strengthened when we realised that we shared a love of the emerging genre of industrial music and of The Residents. Now I was having holes in my musical education filled. Nag had a great collection of dub reggae. Both Nag and Igor had loads of little known punk singles, and Igor had a few weird experimental discs. One of these was a cheaply put together album called Grey Scale by David Cunningham. A small ensemble plays repetitive phrases over and over. If someone makes a mistake then they had to keep repeating that mistake, so that gradually the music changes. I liked both the repetition and the cybernetic rules. Igor introduced me to the word cybernetic. He may have learned it from a lecture by Eno (that he had attended with Nag wearing a gorilla mask).

Mention of his name led to them showing me some of the Obscure Records that Eno had produced. Each one had the same picture of an urban landscape on the cover – but mostly obscured with black ink. Each album had a different shaped "window" where part of the original colourful cover was revealed. The albums they played me were modern "classical" music – or at least with orchestral instruments. On Gavin Bryars' "Jesus Blood Never Failed Me Yet" a recording of a tramp singing a few lines of a hymn is repeated many times, over the backdrop of a melancholy orchestral score. Christopher Hobbs' Aran featured what sounded like a clockwork orchestra playing gongs and bells.

And there were more in this series for next time!

That evening we went for a drink at The Railway Tavern in Crouch End. Everyone was talking about the election. Would a Tory victory make people more depressed and more angry and thus make a revolution more likely? No, people were more militant under a Labour government... I felt naïve and listened more than I contributed. The local font of wisdom was a man called Alan Harrison, in his 30's wearing a suit and a trilby, involved in managing left field bands and producing art magazines. Name anything and he had been there, done that. We talked until gone closing time. The barman said – if you really don't want to go home, there's an extension on at the Queen's Hotel tonight. So a small bunch of us wandered down to the Queen's. Igor decided to carry on home, but Nag and I went in for another drink.

The Queen's was a huge Irish pub. There was a band playing, accommodating floor singers. Nag and I offered to sing and when the band asked what tune, Nag said - play a twelve bar. Neither he nor I knew what that meant. But the band played and we spontaneously improvised an insulting song about Margaret Thatcher, somehow alternating lines and rhyming with each other, then repeating anything that sounded successfully funny or nasty. The audience applauded – for our political stance if not our musicality.

We finished our drinks and set off home. Rather than spit on the window of the Conservative Party shopfront, we went in. There was a crowd of party volunteers watching the election results starting to come in on telly. We explained that we had done some campaigning work, and there was someone there to verify this. We milled around long enough to steal a bottle of whiskey and set off for home again. En route, we passed the Labour party local HQ and decided to pop in on them as well. People there also were watching the election results. Nag whispered to me – lets nick that typewriter. I tried to quietly explain to him that his drunken attempt at a whisper was loud enough for people to hear, and that he was being watched. I apologised for his drunkenness on his behalf and walked him home. I dumped him in bed and got Igor to come back out with me. I showed him the bottle of whiskey and explained that we could possibly pocket some drinks at the Labour HQ. So back we went. The drinks were actually thin on the ground and the Labour supporters were drinking beer rather than spirits, but we helped ourselves to a heap of vote Labour t shirts. We dumped these at home, and then set off searching for the Liberal Party offices. We had no idea where these might be, but thought that we should treat all three parties with equal contempt. By the time we finally found them, the Liberals were closing up for the night.

We awoke the next day to nurse our hangovers and to face the prospect of Margaret Thatcher and a Conservative government. And Rossi retained his seat!

Snotcher

Just before I moved to London, Nag had come to stay with me and my parents for a few days in Swindon. My parents were reassured that although he had an odd name he seemed pleasant enough, and my brother had enjoyed playing about on the Wasp. I'd introduced Nag to an old school friend of mine called Joy and she had fallen in love with him. Now she came to stay at weekends and they would spend lots of time in bed together. When Nag wanted privacy our front room was unavailable. I would play in the rehearsal room or read in my bedroom. I was keeping a diary, full of existential worrying about what I was up to and the meaning of my activity. And I was jealous of Nag – I wanted someone to share my bed too!

My feelings about Joy getting together with Nag were mixed. I'd always fancied her myself, and she'd always deflected me saying that we should be "just friends". So, I was initially jealous of him, but liked keeping a connection in London with at least one old friend. As she got more familiar with Igor and with our house she gradually became more motherly, or something, telling us we should be cleaning more frequently, and generally trying to manage our housekeeping. Slowly Igor and I began to begrudge her presence.

My brother also came to visit. He was bemused by being addressed as Snotcher by my flatmates, but that was a name he had used to communicate with SIC and it stuck. I too took to calling him Snotcher. Interestingly, when he had first signed his name that way, he had put (long for snot) in brackets after it. Now on his visits to the capital, he asked me how could I live in such a dirty place? He bemoaned what I had quickly grown used to – that when you blew your nose, your snot was black. Inspired by the ideas of SIC he had gotten rolls of stickers printed. All they said was: This sticker is removable. They were good for attaching to anything from which they were not easily removable.

We acquired a cat. Ade gave us a little female kitten that had been left abandoned. We decided that Nag should call her Igor, that Igor would call her Bendle and that I would call her Nag. After a few days this got changed to just calling her Ad Hoc. Igor was the least keen that we adopt a kitten, and he became less keen when she pissed on his albums. Nag's records were stacked next to Igor's, but only Igor's were urinated upon. As she grew into a huge beautiful long haired cat she developed two mean habits. If people stroked her she would purr and fuss and then suddenly claw at the person stroking her. She had a knack of catching a claw on the septum of people's noses and making them bleed. She would also attack Igor. Igor was not a morning person. Sometimes we'd urge him out of bed to take a phone call, and he would come downstairs wrapped in his duvet. Ad Hoc would detect his vulnerability and claw viciously at his bare feet.

Igor and I decided that we should grow vegetables. We dug over the lawn in the back garden and planted a few vegetable seeds.

Blue Screaming were playing a gig in a youth centre in Southgate. Nag and I went to hear them. The first band on was called Moorgate and the Tube Disasters. They were a bunch of schoolkids trying to act like their idea of nasty punk musicians. Part way through their set the singer produced a pig's head from a bag and held it up to the audience. And then he threw it at the audience. Some people were offended, some were pissed off at getting splashed with blood. Someone threw the head back at the band and general fighting broke out. The management turned on all the lights and broke up the fights and decided that the evening should be stopped. If this was just the first band, how bad would things get later on? Despite the protestations from the other two bands on the bill, that was the end of the evening. Nag and I helped the disgruntled members of Blue Screaming to put away their gear. Chris, their drummer, demanded to know what the singer of the other band – a mod revival group – intended to convey by wearing a union jack t shirt – was he some kind of fascist? The singer sheepishly explained that it was just "mod style".

Nag's parents, Betty and Michael lived in Southgate, and they would regularly invite me round for dinner on a Sunday. They were a Jewish family, who didn't actively pursue their faith, but celebrated some of the festivals to which they would also invite me and Igor as well. After a Sunday meal I would educate myself by reading Betty's feminist Spare Rib magazines. Whereas I felt I couldn't discuss much about my life with my own parents, I was impressed with Nag's openness with his and enjoyed talking with them, especially Betty.

Igor had an idea: art graffiti. He suggested that we make large stencils and that if we each had one stencil and one colour paint spray we could quickly make guerrilla murals on walls. In the wake of Southall he suggested we could do a picture of an SPG officer hitting a Rasta with a truncheon. We bought some cheap spray paint and started to cut stencils out of large bits of cardboard. Nag and I decided to try a more simple design first with just two colours. We went out at night and sprayed our paint onto the library wall at Crouch End, and signed it with a stencil of the SIC symbol. It was rubbish. The colours we had chosen hardly showed up on the brickwork. We dumped the stencil and started to walk home. But whilst we had the paint, why not graffiti our band name on a wall? There was a hoarding all around the YMCA in Tottenham Lane which we used as our noticeboard. Working backwards from a shady area into full street-light illumination, we had written: *And The Window* when we were interrupted. A car screeched to a halt and three muscled guys in t shirts and fourth in a string vest jumped out and grabbed us. I thought we were in for a severe beating, and I was actually relieved when one of them announced that they were police. They bundled us into the car and took us to the local police station a few hundred yards away. The station was close enough that two of the plain clothes officers walked back since there was not room in the car. We were searched and questioned. I had the SIC logo stencil in my pocket and they wanted to know where that had been used, so, to Nag's dismay, I admitted to the library graffiti as well. They said they would investigate, and set a date for us to return in a fortnight to see if we would be charged or not.

I awoke in the middle of that night with my jaw locked together. This had been happening every now and again since I had moved to London. I would be unable to open my mouth and would have to gently ease my jaw apart with my hands. It scared me but I didn't mention it to anyone. I guessed that it was a delayed reaction to fear of violence at Matlock – where my bedroom door had been kicked in several times in the night, and I had been attacked – but my intellectual understanding didn't make it go away.

Matlock

My teachers at school had correctly predicted that I would only get two good "A" level results. My qualifications wouldn't get me into university. Therefore, they suggested, I should apply to teacher training college. The idea appealed to my parents and numbly I proceeded as directed. I decided that I wanted to study ecology as my main subject, but there were only two colleges in the whole country offering anything like that. There was one course in Environmental Science in Southampton, and at Matlock a course called Ecology and Geography. After an interview, I was offered a place at Matlock. The location appealed to me because of the Peak District countryside.

I'd spent some of the summer after my exams working in a factory processing mailouts of catalogues and subscription magazines. These arrived in the factory on pallets wrapped in large sheets of overprinted paper. I had collected some of these sheets upon which pages from children's storybooks had been printed on top of different sized pages from an engineering manual, and parts of a billboard advert. Arriving at Matlock I put these random collages up as posters in my shared room in college accommodation. My room-mate arrived half an hour later and put up a football league table chart. Within an hour of my arrival I'd already been marked as a weirdo. This was compounded when I tried to share my taste in music with the other residents of the shared house. On my part I was instantly bitterly disappointed – I had an image of students as being free-thinking liberal intellectuals, but all the boys seemed to be rugby and football fans with very mainstream cultural views. My room-mate was studying sport and had permed hair. The girls in their segregated accommodation seemed to all be attached to boyfriends back in their home towns.

During our induction week I found that only one other person had applied to do the course I had applied for. It was explained to us that they would sort something out long term, but for the first year we would be studying the biology and geography modules, and that for the first year biology was all about ecology. As part of our social induction we were offered a coach trip out to a club in Sheffield. The venue turned out to be a cavernous disco playing chart pop songs. All the boys got drunk and tried to chat up the girls who were being faithful to the boys back home. I sat on the steps outside and chatted to a girl from the college who held the event in as much contempt as me.

The girls' accommodation was mostly in a large building that had been a hotel back when Matlock and Matlock Bath had been attractive destinations as spa towns. The boys were divided amongst a series of smaller buildings. I was in a place called Stoneycroft which housed just under 20 of us in shared rooms of 2 -3 beds. There was a mix of boys from each year of study in the house. For all students it seemed to be compulsory to use an empty Mateus Rose wine bottle as a candlestick holder. I dirtied a fat white candle and stuck it in a grubby milk bottle.

I quickly discovered that there was a small village atmosphere in both Stoneycroft and in the college, with a fear of anything that strayed from the norm. Early on in my first term someone announced that another first year, dubbed Toerag, seemed to be behaving oddly. He needs a bath – suggested one of the third years. A bath was filled with cold water and Toerag grabbed and wrestled into the water fully clothed. To my shame I helped dunk him in. I subsequently apologised to him and he refused to take part when I was the second victim a few days later.

I attended my lectures, feeling ambivalent about the geography, but was keen on what I was learning of ecology. I carefully budgeted my grant, and spent only frugally, which allowed me to buy the guitar when I went to visit Garry in Grimsby. From a local army surplus store I bought my NATO jacket and a greatcoat. The latter was practical for the bitter winter weather, but more romantically my purchase was inspired by the words of a Syd Barrett song: *moving around in a trenchcoat with the satin entrail...*

Visiting Garry for a weekend and meeting him for the first time I felt I was being true to what I really wanted to do. I bought the electric guitar from a second hand shop and played it through an amplifier of Garry's accompanied by his drumming – he had a full kit in his bedroom in the house where he lived with his parents. We swopped musical roles and made up words for songs. I caught the train back to Matlock full of inspiration and hope for the future. Arriving back at Stoneycroft I was mocked for my aspirations to become a "rock star". They couldn't know just how much contempt I had for the idea of "rock stars".

One evening, half way through the term I was messing about. In an effort to amuse or to confuse the other residents, I said hello to everyone who was watching TV in the front room and went up the stairs to my room. I climbed out of the window, down a drainpipe, and back in through the front door. Said hello in the lounge and ascended the stairs again. Having climbed down the drainpipe I was about to enter the front room again when I overheard plans to "give him a bath" and I swiftly fled. I was aware that the Buzzcocks were playing in Derby that night. I checked in my pocket and reckoned I had enough money to get to the gig on a train and to get in. I didn't have enough money to get home, and no way of getting any cash. I set off for the station.

On the train I met a few locals from Matlock who, as I correctly guessed from their dress, were heading to the same gig. I mentioned to one of them that I didn't know how I'd get home. Stick with us, he said – we've got a minibus booked to take us home, and there'll be room for you. The gig was amazing – the Buzzcocks themselves and also the support act Subway Sect, who I hadn't heard before. Both groups played intense music at a manic rate, and the whole audience bounced around and celebrated. It felt like a huge friendly party. Even the large contingent of skinheads in the audience danced peacefully. The gang of Matlock people chipped in and paid for my share of the bill for an Indian meal, and then took me home in the minibus. They told me their hangout was The Gate pub, a student free hangout. I said I'd see them there. I had a lifeline.

Amongst the student clubs there was one called The Apathy Society. The idea pissed me off. One evening near to Christmas in the student bar, I initiated the removal of posters from the wall and started making large paper planes. People joined in and amidst the chaos of the room being filled with flying paper I took down the Apathy Society poster, rolled it up, and burned it on the way home. Burning things was a way of dealing with what I didn't like. I'd burned the Gideon's Bible that had been left in my room, and I'd been carefully burning the Stoneycroft library, a magazine at a time. The "library" was a collection of porn magazines kept in one of the resident's rooms in a cardboard box. I hated the idea that I was supposed to enthuse about this and to discuss sex in a particular way just by virtue of my gender. This was before I'd read Betty's Spare Rib magazines and I had no idea of sexual politics, but I hated anything that encouraged lack of thinking and mob mentality.

Returning to college after Christmas I had a visitor to my room. A burly 4th year came in and told me I was a marked man. I'd been seen burning the Rugby Club poster. Watch out, he warned me, and - Now you've done it! added my room mate. I had no awareness of the Rugby Club poster. I admitted what I had actually done to Toerag and his room-mate Andy, and Andy helped me draft a replacement poster for the Apathy Society.

I decided to keep a low profile. I'd try to get to meals in the college canteen either very early or very late. I avoided any college get togethers or the college bar, and spent more time with my new friends at the Gate. But I seemed to have a knack for being in the wrong place, and for doing or saying things that would be taken wrongly. Out for a pub crawl a couple of students from Stoneycroft came into the Gate and one said – So this is where you hang out, is it? And I failed to stifle my involuntary response of: Fuck off. I was overheard playing along on my guitar with a Chain of Dots piece. I was discovered to be the person making discordant music on the piano in the music room – where I shouldn't have been. I got drunk with two other students and joined with them in smashing up some furniture in their room. The postcards that Nag sent, urging me to move to London, were read by the others before I got to see them. I instructed him to use envelopes!

I nearly managed to upset the regulars of The Gate, too. Their jukebox included a copy of *Hong Kong Garden* by Siouxsie and the Banshees. I selected the B side – *Voices*. No one in the pub liked this wailing noise except for me. Someone kicked the jukebox to knock it forward – but the stylus jumped back. Each time someone kicked the machine they inadvertently extended the song's duration.

In the college I spent more time around the girl's halls of residence. Any romantic advances I made were rejected, but the girls were safer to be around. There was a curfew time by which boys were meant to be out of the building, but I found that the caretaker was a hippyish guy a few years older than me who would let me in, or with whom I'd sit chatting in the boiler room.

A snowball fight happened between a neighbouring student house and ours. I hesitated to join in, worried about making my position worse, nervously moulding and remoulding the snowball in my hands. Finally I threw it, realising that I'd hit the captain of the Rugby Club in the face with what was now an iceball. I ran off, but a while later realised I was being searched for. I overheard someone say that if they found me they would tie me naked to a rugby goal post and leave me there. Scared stiff I hid in the bedroom of one of the rugby players thinking it the safest place to be.

A few nights later my bedroom door was kicked open in the night and I was held by two students and thumped by a third whilst being told I was the sort of student who brought the college into disrepute. And then I was thrown into a cold bath into which several boys had pissed and one had shat. The students who attacked me were third and fourth years, soon to qualify and take their places of leadership in classrooms and sports fields.

I tried to struggle on with my studies. I was sure that had I gone to university to study I would hardly have been noticed. I was small, didn't dress conspicuously, and my taste in music affected no-one. But Matlock College was a nasty small minded little place. Scared to make the decision to leave, I initially planned a year off from study.

Just before the Easter holidays Toerag, another student called Simon and me were mucking about throwing unwanted items out of bedroom windows. We went down into the garden to tidy up and I threw a glass saucer like a frisbee. The wind caught it and it sailed off much further than intended. We heard it smash some way off. Later that evening we had a visit from the college Principal. Who had thrown the saucer? I admitted it, the other two kindly said they were also responsible. He said that he wanted to see the three of us in his room the next morning. The (flying) saucer had apparently crashed through the skylight of a toilet in the offices of an architect, in a property some way down the road.

I fretted and fretted. Toerag pointed out that the Principal was just using standard stress induction tactics – make them stew 'til tomorrow. He said - Listen, he's just a bloke right, and you're just a bloke, and we're just going to have a chat. What's the worst he can do? Throw you out? You'd be glad to be out of this place!

The next morning the three of us endured our admonishment, quietly, yes sir, no sir. I thought it was over, but Simon said – But you don't know the pressures we're under, that cause us to let off steam in stupid ways. Take Bendle, for instance – (no, don't, I said inwardly, please don't) – he's been pulled from his bed and thrown into a cold bath... The Principal turned to me and said directly: But you burned the Rugby club poster!

Shopping

Once a week the three of us would walk to Wood Green Shopping Centre, to do our shopping at a big branch of Sainsbury's and at a few stalls selling veg. Usually we would each chip in £4 and that would be enough to buy most of our week's groceries, and we would struggle home with a couple of heavy bags each. On top of this we would each put a pound into a kitty for milk and bread which we would buy throughout the week, nearer to home. We relied upon cheap staples like spuds and onions and tins of tomatoes, but every now and again would be tempted to buy some expensive treats like fresh mushrooms or to spend too much of our budget on meat. Once we spent most of our budget on a bottle of whiskey, some yoghurt and a tin of condensed milk.

We had a discussion about becoming vegetarian. Given that mostly we subsisted on vegetarian curries, this didn't seem like a hard challenge to take on board. For ethical reasons I had discussed this idea with my parents in Swindon a couple of years earlier. They just flatly refused to accommodate the idea of the expense of cooking different food for me. I had responded by buying my own wholemeal flour and making my own bread for my last years at home, feeling like this was a move in the right direction.

We set out to the supermarket with the aim of buying only vegetarian products, carefully reading the list of ingredients on everything that would normally go into our basket. Loads of things seemed to have animal fat in them. By the time we got to the last aisle of the shop we had very little in our trolley apart from some tins of tomatoes, a tube of tomato purée and some pasta. We concluded that our mission was unachievable, and re-navigating the store, filled our trolley with our usual products.

Ethically we had an urge to abstain from meat, but emotionally there was an attraction to eating it. If we returned home after a gig via Turnpike Lane tube, we had to avoid the lure of several Cypriot kebab shops along Turnpike Lane. To keep up our resolve the three of us would chant – Refuse to buy a kebab, refuse to buy a kebab...

LMC

At some point in 1978 there had been an article in one of the mainstream music papers mentioning the Los Angeles Free Music Association, and closer to home, the London Musicians Collective. The LMC produced a magazine called Musics, and I had ordered a couple of copies. They contained obscure articles on obscure music. There were pictures of men in boats playing music on (and to?) the Grand Union Canal, and there was mention of the LMC having a building where gigs were put on. I urged my flatmates to investigate the LMC. We found that they had monthly meetings, and that if you joined the collective that you could rent the space as a venue for next to nothing.

The LMC building was in Gloucester Avenue in Camden – we got there by walking along the tow path of the canal from Camden High Street. The place was a dusty warehouse-like space on the first floor, accessed from the street by a flight of iron steps. In the front door, either turn left and there was another door for the Film Makers Coop, or turn right and you were in the LMC. We attended a meeting, which was very dull – a little discussion about the building and its maintenance, and quite a lot of talk about getting funding from the Arts Council, both for the organisation, and for individual performances. We joined. There was a message pinned on a noticeboard that a pianist called Akemi Kuniyoshi wanted another act to play with her in a few weeks' time. We took the number, phoned her and got ourselves on the bill.

We rehearsed at home for our Mayhem gig. We tried to reproduce some of the tunes on our EP and were undeterred by our inability to faithfully replicate them. We noted down Wasp settings and worked out a way of notating what I was doing with the guitar. I refused to learn to tune the guitar in any orthodox way – I just had a vague idea of what seemed right to me. We recorded backing tracks onto my clunky reel to reel recorder. We rewrote lyrics inspired by our improvised ones in the rehearsal studio, and started to write new songs as well. Despite ourselves we found that we were developing a rhythmic pulse to the pieces that we were learning. We never played anything exactly the same twice, but we both had a sense of what a song title implied, and each had an idea of what the other one should be doing. And once we recorded a backing track we had a reference point or an anchor to hold onto.

We planned on performing naked, or just wearing see-through plastic bags, but when it came to the event we were both too shy. We were both jittery with stage fright. Somehow I was the one to check that all the amps were switched on and that things were wired up and ready to go. Nag's nervousness caused him to be unable to do anything useful, but it served me well, since I was distracted from my own fear by having to concentrate on practicalities. There was a modest crowd at Mayhem and they actually applauded after each tune. We got through a whole set without any fights and without being pulled from the stage by bouncers! The hardest bit was when the Wasp started playing itself for a while. We realised that the touch sensitive keyboard would go wrong if Nag's fingers were damp.

We enjoyed Blue Screaming's performance, but it was to be their last. Igor no longer wanted to be in a pop band – he was developing ideas for something more with more lofty political and philosophical aspirations – but only one of the current band shared his enthusiasms.

For our gig at the LMC we would have no PA. We decided to get around this by recording the vocal parts of our songs onto the backing tape. We took our gear to the venue in a black taxi cab and set up our speakers. We didn't meet Akemi until the night of the gig. She was a very friendly Japanese woman of indeterminate age, who seemed to be bossed about by her managerial English husband. He was suspicious of us, and seemed to dislike the fact that we were using amplification.

Ami suggested that we each play two sets – with her playing first, because she preferred the idea of loud after quiet. It seemed that she had produced no publicity for the event at all. We had duplicated some A4 handouts and left them in local venues and shops such as Compendium Books. We gathered an audience of six or seven people, which we learned with dismay was the usual audience size for the venue. Akemi played what I guessed to be noodly jazz. We applauded mutedly and we ourselves played rather self-consciously in the gloomy space. Our words were unintelligible through the guitar amp. One of the audience members was a bespectacled thirty-something bloke who introduced himself to us in the interval as Steve Beresford, one of the key members of the Collective. He enthused about our noise and especially about my naïve approach to the guitar – don't EVER learn to play it, he directed.

We found that it was usual practice at the LMC to adjourn to The Engineer, the pub across the road, for intervals between sets. Partly this was necessary because there was no proper toilet in the building. All the performers and the small audience moved out and we locked the door for 20 minutes, then we announced the second half and we all made our way back again.

It all seemed a bit silly, playing for a handful of people and our hearts weren't in it. We split the pitiful door money and worked out how much we had lost on taxi fares. But we diligently began to attend the monthly LMC meetings and we booked more evenings at the venue.

Peel

Early in June I celebrated my 19th birthday and soon after that we had our 1st single ready. Excitedly we unboxed the singles and stuck the white sleeves into our wrap-around yellow card covers. When they were all done I kept opening one of the boxes and taking another proud look – we'd made a single! We made a list of distribution companies and phoned them to arrange meetings to sell our music. Rough Trade was one of our first visits. There were friendly faces behind the counter of the (small) shop – Steve and Sue and Pete, whom we knew from being customers. We were shown through the shop to the offices at the back. We sat silently, knotted up inside whilst our music was listened to by fuzzy-haired Geoff and another bloke. Would they hate it or would they say it was ok? They would take 200 copies! We were jubilant.

Rough Trade seemed to be the epicentre of an excited and exciting wave of young people producing their own music and records. The shop itself was tiny but was always busy, and we'd often meet other musicians. Today Daniel Miller, whom we knew to be the man using the aka The Normal, was hanging around the shop, so we got to say hello to him. We chatted for a while, Daniel holding a tin of coke in one hand, and a cigarette in the other, tapping the fag ash into the tin. He finished his cigarette, and popped the butt into the tin, and absent-mindedly took a swig of his coke!

Psi came with us on some of our marketing meetings. At the offices of Fresh Records – which were in someone's front room – he did a weird belly dance to our music, whilst Nag and I looked on in horror. Despite this Fresh bought some as well. We were expecting people to give us money, but instead they said we should invoice them. They would pay us in a month.

We sent letters to the music papers and got little mentions in the news columns that our single was available by mail order directly from NB Records. We sent copies off for review, and set off for the BBC to get a copy to John Peel. His late evening radio show on Radio 1 was the only place where adventurous music might get national exposure.

There seemed to be only one main entrance to the big BBC building in Portland Place, so we hung around there from late afternoon and collared John Peel as he entered. He was unbothered at being accosted by two scruffy young men brandishing their DIY single. He told us that, before punk, record company executives would take him out for a drink. Post-punk he seemed to take the artists out for a drink – would we like to come with him? He took us into the building and up to his studio, introduced us to his producer, John Walters, dealt with a few things that required his attention and then took us to a nearby bar. He bought us a pint each and one for himself and charmed us with some anecdotes about recent visitors to his studio. Then, explaining that he had a low tolerance to alcohol, declined our offer to buy him a drink. He bought us a second pint each and he went back to work and then we went home to tune in and hear him play one of our tracks that evening. We were on the radio!

Igor had started a new band called Take It – just him playing organ and Simon from Blue Screaming playing guitar, both singing. Several times a week they would rehearse, alternating their use of the rehearsal room with Nag and I. We tried to be considerate of the neighbours, and said that we would be quiet in the evenings, but the people on one side of us worked from home and complained sporadically about the din. Picking up my guitar Simon pointed out that my tuning seemed to be getting some consistency. It wasn't conventional in any way, he said, but I obviously had an idea of what sounded right to me.

Steve From Finchley, as he was known to Nag and Igor, came to visit the three of us with his mates Heman and John. This was the Steve who had met me at the Crypt in Paddington. Nag and Igor knew him as someone with an encyclopaedic knowledge of obscure music, especially Krautrock. He had provided us with mix tapes of bands that we would not otherwise have heard. Now he and his friends (under the name of Nurse With Wound) had been recording an album of their own stuff, and came to talk over the doing of noise and music. With NB Records Nag and I had just registered the name of the business. Steve was planning bigger and had set up a limited company. The cheapest way to do this, he explained, was to buy the name of a business that had gone bust. He proudly announced that his label was called United Dairies!

Steve brought with him some music making gear that he thought we might like to borrow for a while. This included an old drum machine (with buttons labelled waltz, two step, march, etc. with which interesting rhythms could be produced by jamming in two buttons at once); a contact microphone, and a metal rack designed to hold albums but which worked as a good sound source amplified via the contact mic. We gratefully added these items to our armoury of junk instruments.

Our radio exposure brought us more offers of performing, including a gig in Maldon in Essex, which we accepted on condition that we could use amps borrowed from the headline act. This meant that we could travel on the train lugging just our instruments. Between the sound-check and our performance, we got chatting with the young brother of the promoter, who introduced himself as Grevious, and who offered to play drums with us. The band who's gear we were using said yes to us utilising their drumkit as well, so with no rehearsal, we adopted a drummer for the night.

The headline band was a neo-mod outfit, and the audience we mostly mods. We were scared of them, but they seemed more scared of us, standing well back from the front of the stage. In our song called Religion, I had a bible which I tore up. My intention was to throw pages at the audience, but because they were keeping their distance, I had to rip it into big chunks. Ranting and taunting the audience I felt simultaneously powerful and scared stiff. My insistence all through my teens upon following my heart and standing out from the crowd had consistently been punished by violence. Here I was making myself even more visible, but I felt empowered by the volume of noise we were creating. Grevious pounded some awful 4/4 rock band rhythms in the background, and the three of us did our best to be in synch with each other and the backing tape. Most of the audience hated us, but not violently. We saw the gig as another success, and were interviewed as soon as we left the stage by a bloke from a local fanzine.

We got reviews of the single in the music papers and we started to sell copies by mail order. We also started to receive a steady flow of unsolicited and unwanted demo tapes. People seemed to think we were a real record company, and wanted us to put their music out. Lots of the tapes just contained horrible noise. We took to fast forwarding them, and if they sounded the same 10 minutes in as they did at the beginning, would just put them in a pile to be re-used. As well as getting demo tapes from far flung places, we also started to receive singles from bands and small labels from all around the world. We suddenly and quite organically began to be part of a large undefined network.

We suddenly seemed very popular in South Devon – we started getting first mail order requests and then fan letters from a bunch of teenage boys who we assumed all went to school together. We spray painted some of our collection of "Vote Labour" t shirts with doodles and sent them off as free gifts. People who sent us cheques or postal orders for our single would often get some sort of free gift with their order.

Eyebrow

In the middle of June Nag and I were before Highgate Magistrates Court, charged with criminal damage relating to our arrest for graffiti. A few days beforehand Igor had suggested that the three of us shave off our eyebrows. We all egged each other on and then agreed to each initially shave one off. The other two decided that the lack of one eyebrow was weird enough and stuck at removing one. I thought I'd look less strange if my face was symmetrical, and shaved off both of my eyebrows. On the day of going to court Nag borrowed my reading glasses to hide his missing eyebrow. I faced the magistrate looking odd. We both said we were sorry. We were fined £20 each – which suddenly got upped to £35 when the clerk pointed out to the magistrate that the fine was too small! £35 was what I got every two weeks from the dole, including my rent. The court knew that we were unemployed and said that we could pay £5 per week. We wondered how we would get by for 7 weeks.

Two days later we started making our first film. The project was Giblet's idea, and he roped in his mate Crispen to help. Filmed over three days on an old Super 8 camera, the concept was to make a surreal goody versus baddie film. I was the baddie, dressed in black, but at the end I morphed into the goodie, and Nag, who had been the goodie, dressed in white morphed into the baddie. Most of my evil acts are only hinted at in the film, apart from a shot of me stealing fruit from a veg seller's barrow and smashing it on the floor. Giblet's title for the film was Nostalgia Dribble, and the production was credited to Kebab and Chips at the Acropolis. The plot was partly directed by the props that we found in skips and bins. Lacking any resources to edit the film we needed to film the scenes in the order they would be shown. We liked the idea of trying some stop frame animation, and although it had nothing to do with the plot we did manage to animate an old child's doll at the end of the film. She walks a few steps and kicks over a milk bottle.

Giblet had just finished school. We'd met up a couple of times since our first meeting. I'd gone to see the Pop Group and Good Missionaries with him and he had heckled some boring performers who were doing an agit-prop thing about the SUS laws, and I had seen him play a gig at the Dublin Castle in his band, Buddy Hernia and the

Rickets. Buddy was a shop dummy propped at the front of the stage. The band played Giblet's songs but their aspirations towards heavy rock made me feel I'd have preferred seeing him solo.

One evening Giblet had come to visit the three of us in Ferrestone Road with tapes of the BBC radio play *The Hitch Hiker's Guide to the Galaxy*, and we mangled our brains by listening to the whole series in one evening. He tried to follow this up on other evenings by playing us his albums by The Firesign Theatre, but we were less impressed by this Goons-like American comedy.

Not knowing quite what to do with it myself, I presented Giblet with the SIC folder and told him that he now had his own organisation to (mis)manage. A year younger than me, Giblet knew lots more about music and art and art history than me. He explained that the idea of noise as music was much older than I appreciated. He showed me pictures of the intonamuri made by Luigi Russolo and a copy of Russolo's manifesto The Art of Making Noises published in 1913.

Walking through central London with Giblet, I was accosted by a Hari Krishna devotee who invited us to a free meal in their Soho temple, and failing to sell me a record, gave me a copy, telling me that I was a compassionate person and that I would benefit from listening to it. A little further on I realised that I had walked ahead of Giblet. Looking back I saw him talking with two men whom I assumed were friends of his parents. I walked back to them and tried to sell them the Hari Krishna album, asking, in an American accent – Would you like to take a listen to our album? – It's produced by George Harrison and any profit that we - Push off – I was interrupted by one of the men. Both of them were plain clothes policemen. They had stopped my friend because of the surrealist poetry written in large letters on his white trousers – what did it mean?

I'd begun to realise that I could get to meet people in the same way Giblet had met us – by recognising kindred spirits at gigs. Go and see the Gang of Four or The Raincoats and there would be familiar faces in the audience. Some places needed money to get in, but I began to learn that at some venues – like the student union buildings at North London Poly and ULU in Central London – that I could turn up early, wander in during the soundcheck, and then hide in the toilets when they cleared the hall of freeloaders, emerging when the paying audience was entering.

Nag and I did our next gig at the LMC – but not as a TDATW gig. We joined forces with Simon Leonard and Psi, and did a performance with the four of us playing. We positioned ourselves in the four corners of the darkened room and the small audience wandered in between us. Psi was normally mostly drawn to playing pop and rock on his home-made guitar. He could play things like songs by the Beetles, but was keen to experiment with what he called concrete music. Nag and Psi and I tried to listen to each other and to build some sort of music together, but Simon seemed oblivious to anyone else's contribution and did what he wanted in his corner. The experiment felt to me like a failure.

The Sound of Music

Giblet somehow got booked onto a slot for new bands at the trendy upmarket venue Dingwalls and asked Nag and me if we'd like to do the gig with him. His name for the band was Repetition and the Repetitions and his proposal was that we perform the whole of The Sound of Music. It seemed like a good idea to us so we set to rehearsing - with two guitars, the drum machine and Nag's Wasp. For some of the songs we kept the original words, others needed rewriting – *burning down bridges and pulling flies' wings, these are a few of my favourite things* – and we were ready to go. Giblet pointed out that it was a story of timeless appeal – nuns versus Nazis!

Chris, the drummer who had played with Blue Screaming, had a job as a cook. He helped to feed us whilst our funds were depleted by way of our fine payments. He came by with a bucket of chicken livers. Igor had found a crate of red peppers left behind after a street market, and for a week or so all our meals were made of these two ingredients. On the night of the Dingwalls gig Chris provided us with two huge cheesecakes. We thought we'd undermine Dingwalls policy of selling overpriced food by giving away free slices of cheesecake.

We sang our first few songs with some interest from the audience, but the stage manager didn't seem to like us. He turned the stage lights off. When we carried on regardless, he turned the PA off. We carried on singing. The DJ started to play a record over the top of us and a few people objected, so the DJ asked over the PA – OK, it's over to you, the audience - can you take another 20 minutes of this crap? Surprisingly, to him and to us, the audience's response was a resounding yes. So with both the lights and the PA switched back on we got to continue with our story whilst Psi and Chris and Igor and Dolores (whose name we had sung at the Nashville rooms) gave away slices of cheesecake to the audience. We got enough applause at the end for us to do an encore of *All Things Bright and Beautiful*, with new words improvised on the spot. We also got a long and enthusiastic review the following week in Record Mirror!

Later in the evening as we were moving our equipment, Nag was stopped by one of the Dingwall's bouncers – a huge bloke that we had dubbed Sperm Whale. Are you the keyboard player? When Nag affirmed that he was, Sperm Whale said – if I ever see you in here again I'll break all your fingers and you'll never play a keyboard again.

We'd arranged a gig the following night at the LMC. Dingwalls was on the side of the canal, and we'd intended to carry our amps and speakers a few hundred metres along the tow-path and up the steps to the LMC and leave them there overnight. But the gate to the tow-path was locked for the night, so Nag, Giblet, Psi and I had to take the long way round by road. There was too much stuff for us to carry, so we would walk a little way, put things down and go back to collect the rest.

Having mocked the Dingwalls aesthetic, we were out to do the same to that of the LMC. We were performing under the name of The Liberated Sound Octet. There were five of us – Psi, Chris, Giblet, Nag and me. We'd attended a few of the evenings that happened at the venue and felt we had a handle on how to do a spoof of a free improvised performance. Our main instrument for part of the evening was to be a piano keyboard with no strings. Our pitifully sized audience included an LMC stalwart - Max Eastley, who enjoyed our sense of humour and enthused about our performance.

Travel

If we caught the overground from Hornsey station, it would pause for a while at Highbury and Islington whilst the power source was changed over from overhead cables to a third rail under the train. The lights on the train would flicker for a moment, and Nag would say: London Plane. He reckoned these were two things that I had taught him – the name of a tree and the power supply of a train, and now he would use one to name the other. On his part he showed me how to get around on London's transport system paying as little money as possible. I'd still try to buy half fares, but didn't always succeed. Nag got away with it less often than me. So he helped me to learn which stations had emergency stair exits – which would mean we could dodge the ticket inspector. This might mean a longer walk at our destination, but time was easier to come by than money. I learned that King's Cross underground station was divided into two parts, that flashing an out of date ticket quickly at an inspector and stating that I was going to the lines in the other half meant I could get off there to visit Simon and Psi. Sometimes from home we would walk to the tube at Wood Green and buy a ticket to Turnpike Lane. When we came home later that day we would get off at Turnpike Lane and give in the ticket from earlier.

I also had to get to know the safety of various tube stations. The Angel was somewhere you could get off without showing a ticket, but was a hangout for fascist skinheads, and a dangerous place to pass through. Even on our home turf we needed a degree of wariness. Walking home one evening from Turnpike Lane with Igor and Nag we noted that a bunch of eight or nine blokes seemed to be trailing after us. Run – shouted Igor, and the three of us ran for the next quarter of a mile, until it seemed that our would be assailants had dropped back from running after us.

For most of my teen years I had escaped from the threat of violence that seemed to be ever present in human interactions by exploring the countryside. Either on my own or with one trusted friend I had started to teach myself the names of wild flowers and birds. In London I liked to go to the big parks like Hampstead Heath, but felt hemmed in there. Sometimes I needed real countryside, so I began to take little breaks away from the capital by hitch hiking further afield. I'd head up to Hendon and stick out my thumb and work my way up the M1. A couple of times I'd vanish for a day or two. Once I headed North then across to Birmingham, then down to the Severn Bridge. After wandering around there for a while I hitched to Swindon and spent the night with my parents. Nag would also vanish for a day or two. He went to Sheffield and turned up unexpectedly at the home of Chris Watson from a band called Cabaret Voltaire – but there was no one home. He travelled on to visit people in Manchester.

At Hampstead Heath I wandered around looking at the plants and wildlife. I swam in a couple of the ponds. Several times I bumped into blokes who got chatting to me, and who seemed to get quite quickly very intensely interested in me. I was scared that they were spies from the DHSS. Only slowly did it dawn on me that I fitted some sort of ideal for a particular group of gay men.

Having mentioned to some friends that I'd swum in the ponds at Hampstead they told me that there were proper designated swimming ponds – one male and one female. I went to look for the male one, and found the way into the changing area. It was a hot sunny day and I was astonished to realise that although there was no-one in the pond, the changing area was thronging with naked men, milling about and playing ping pong. I turned and ran.

If I wanted a different environment from home, I'd often pop down to King's Cross and spend time with either Simon or Psi. With Simon I would discuss books and politics and philosophy. He introduced me to the ideas of Ouspensky, and the music of Steve Reich and Philip Glass. With Psi I would drink beer or smoke weed and perhaps go out busking. I'd be a background partner, with Psi playing guitar and the two of us singing anthemic punk pop songs like *Molotov Cocktail*. After Blue Screaming split up he and Chris performed under the name of The Hills Are Alive, playing mostly covers of sixties pop songs. Psi was a weird mix, who would oscillate between ideas that were very conservative and those which were totally oddball.

One time I walked through King's Cross station with him. There were lines painted on the ground to show where queues should align themselves. Looking scruffy and slightly mad, Psi set fire to his hair and walked through the station forecourt yelling at the crowd to get themselves into proper orderly queues – couldn't they see the lines painted at their feet? Several hundred people obeyed his manic shouting. I quietly noted that setting fire to your hair looks dramatic, but is reasonably safe, like burning a pile of dry grass – the flames rush upwards then go out. It seemed like a party trick that I, too might employ.

Friends and Allies

Snotcher came to visit and came with Nag and Giblet and me to see The Swell Maps play at the Nashville Rooms. It was the first time that I had been back there since we had played the venue with Chain of Dots. Nag was frequently being mistaken for Bob Geldof. I'd witnessed a girl run up to him with a Boomtown Rats record and ask him to autograph it. He said – Of course! Then, with the marker pen that she handed him, he scrawled *Nag* in big letters across the front. At the Nashville Rooms, the drummer from the Damned was leaning against the bar. D'you know, he said to Nag – you look just like Bob Geldof? Nag replied: And you look just like Rat Scabies!

It was a great evening – we loved the Swell Maps' singles, a mix of pure frenzied punk chaos, and inept lo-fi bedroom ditties, but this was the first time I'd seen them live. Snotcher loved the gig and was impressed that we knew several members of the band (from Rough Trade). He was a little shocked at how drunk Nag had got, falling in between a tube train and the platform on the way home – I had to haul him out and push him onto the train. He was also surprised at how fondly Nag talked about the violent atmosphere of some of the early punk gigs. Once on the tube Giblet produced his notebook and began to read his poems to the Saturday night crowd:

> If we could build pigs out of plastic
> I know that we would
> Because that is progress...

Surprisingly his tube train audience applauded and called for more, and he entertained our fellow passengers for most of the way home.

A couple of days later, heading home on an overground train with Nag I spotted a couple of nasty looking young men whom I perceived to be a threat. My long history of being on the wrong end of violence and aggression had helped me develop a reasonably accurate radar for trouble. I urged Nag to move along the train, that we weren't safe. When he refused to move I went on my own. When we reconnected on Hornsey station he had been thumped and had had his watch stolen. He seemed less fond of violence.

We were also attacked in Victoria, whilst waiting at a bus stop. Sitting on a wall, with a long drop behind us, we both instinctively jumped down when we saw two bikers get up from seats outside of a pub opposite and make their way towards us. Are you punks? They asked – no. Are you bone heads? Whilst we tried to figure out what a bone head was, they started to hit us with their motorbike helmets. Neither of us knew how to fight. We were doing our best at shielding our heads from their blows when we were rescued by three plain clothes policemen. They wrestled our assailants to the ground and called up a van to take them away. Grilled by a policewoman afterwards, in a police station where we were taken to give statements, she asked what the bikers had said to us. When we reported that they had asked – are you punks? The policewoman recoiled and asked with distaste – you're not are you?

We continued our planned and unplanned connecting with people with similar ideas. I started writing to a boy called Protag from a band called the Instant Automatons, based near Scunthorpe. They were making DIY electronic pop music and releasing albums – only they had decided to circumvent the music business and were putting their recordings out on cassette. You didn't even have to buy them – just send them a blank cassette of the right length and a self-addressed envelope. They would record their album onto the cassette and send it back.

Using the laundrette in Tottenham Lane one day instead of our usual one at the back of the graveyard, I bumped into Cosey Fanni Tutti from Throbbing Gristle. Sitting chatting together whilst we did our washing, I discovered that she and Chris Carter from the band were living together quite close to where Nag and I had been arrested. This in turn was quite close to where the NME journalists Tony Parsons and Julie Birchill were living. We had stuck little TDATW stickers all over the journalists' front door.

I was walking through central London one day with Nag when he spotted Bobo Phoenix, the singer from Dead Fingers Talk. We introduced ourselves as two of the band that had supported DFT at the Nashville Rooms back in January – did he remember us? Yes, he did. In fact he said that he felt that what we had been doing was so raw and unpretentiously honest that he had questioned what he was doing and had subsequently split up his band. Despite the recording contract and everything. There was no point being in a rock band. Did we have time to talk?

He took us back to his little flat above a restaurant in Greek Street in Soho and we listened to him talk in his gentle sing song Hull accent. Had we read Krishnamurti?

The author was a recent discovery of his, and he shared a little of what he understood from his reading. He told us about his life and everything he described sounded like a child excited at discovering something new. His having spent time in prison and his years in a rock band somehow had not blemished his naïve engagement with life. He talked and talked - and he was so keen to hear what we were up to as well. He was still playing music, but just solo stuff. He had a good quality Revox two track recorder and said that we could borrow it to record our second single. He would arrange to get a friend to help him bring it round to our house. We swapped phone numbers and Nag and I bounced up the road together. Bobo was the most inspiring person we'd ever met!

We hadn't gotten paid for all of our sales yet, but in a matter of weeks had sold most of our thousand singles. We were very diligently keeping any NB records money separate from our personal money. The money from the first single would pay for a second. In the long term hopefully we'd be able to pay back Nag's savings.

We did a gig at an Anarchist do in an empty warehouse in Wapping. It was a weird location slightly off of the edge of our map. There was a tube stop there but there seemed to be nothing else. Just empty buildings. The warehouse had been squatted and was filthy – layers of dust and pigeon shit. The band on before us was two blokes – playing a guitar and a little synth, and they had a tape recorder too. They were called The The. We thought they were pale imitations of us! The whole thing was badly organised. It was meant to be an all-night do, but the acts seemed to run out about two in the morning. Using amps supplied by the organisers we had arrived by tube, but there was no way to get home. We tried to settle down and get some rest, but were unable to sleep.

Then around four in the morning another band turned up – there seemed to be loads of them. They were full of energy playing a mangled up mix of all sorts of things - from reggae to sixties pop and easy listening stuff. I was particularly impressed with a woman on drums, a guitarist with the world's longest guitar lead and a scruffy trumpet player. The trumpet player placed a little sign in front of the drum kit – Di Federation. They were buoyantly happy and the semi-comatose audience awoke and many of us started dancing.

At the end of their set I got talking to them – Kathy, the drummer, Roddy the trumpet player and Rob the guitarist. We swapped details and I said I would come visit. They all lived together in an old schoolhouse in Hammersmith. Small rooms there were used as bedrooms and a small hall on the ground floor as an occasional venue. Rob and a guy called Jim (from a band called The Homosexuals) had walked by one day and, seeing the doors open, had walked in. The place drew them and they squatted it and moved in with their friends. Most of the residents were in the band (sometimes), which, it transpired, were called not Di Federation, but The Murphy Federation. Their squat was a great place to visit for inspiration.

In Portobello Road market I bumped into a guy selling copies of a bootleg tape of Alternative TV/ The Good Missionaries (the first band had morphed into the second). The bloke was called Kif Kif, and he ran a little cassette label called Fuck Off Records. I bought a copy of the tape and got talking with him, swapping information on what we both did. He invited TDATW to play at a festival that he was organising – the Bad Music Festival – which would be running over two nights at the Acklam Hall.

Igor came up with the idea of us doing a magazine examining the politics of record production. We'd interview key people about their views on independent labels, signing to majors and so on. Igor had a name for the mag: Common Knowledge. We discussed who we should speak to. The Desperate Bicycles – since they started off the whole new wave DIY scene; Mark Perry because of running the small Deptford Fun City label... Maybe we could we talk to the Clash and how they had failed the possibility of punk changing the world by signing to a major label? The Mekons? We began to explore the possibilities, and slowly to make initial phone calls.

Meanwhile Igor had formed his own little record company called Fresh Hold Releases, and was planning the first Take It single with Simon. They were practising a song with the working title of This is The Stop. But it didn't. They kept repeating it over and over, with its angular stop start rhythms and melodies. It was a great song, but Nag and I were hearing it too often.

One night, about to set off for home after visiting Simon and Psi in Kings X, Simon gave me one of his electric guitars. You need a better guitar, he insisted. You're drunk, I replied. Because he kept insisting, I took it. When he next came round to rehearse a few days later I tried to give it back. I may have been drunk when I gave it to you – he said - but I stand by my words. I gratefully accepted. It was a far better guitar than my crappy little Jedson.

Final Solution, the East End promoters, were putting on four nights at the YMCA in Central London. Four nights of everything that was currently exciting, in a venue not normally used for music events. We couldn't afford all four nights which meant that we missed Thursday night's bill of bands from Manchester and Liverpool. We also missed out on the Saturday gig including Prag Vec and Clock DVA, but Igor, Nag and I were there for the Friday night to see and hear Throbbing Gristle, supported by Cabaret Voltaire. We missed the first band on the bill because we ran into Bobo and got chatting. We were surprised to see him at a gig like this, but talking with him he explained that he knew Genesis from when they both lived in Hull. Together we bumped into Gen in the audience and wandered off to a quiet corner to talk to them. Bobo and Gen were talking about getting older and they discussed the benefits of using avocados as skin conditioners.

Another person whom I was surprised to see in the audience was Patrick Fitzgerald, the so called punk poet. I'd met him very briefly when he had played in Chippenham a year earlier, supporting Here and Now and Alternative TV. I was also surprised that this was his kind of music, but looking around the audience spotted members of all sorts of bands. Patrick and I got talking and exchanged phone numbers.

Cabaret Voltaire seemed very keen on acting aloof and uninterested in the audience. We were disappointed in their performance – they must have had new songs, but they sounded very similar to when we'd heard them at the Crypt. Chris Watson and Nag had been writing to each other and Chris had jokingly asked if they could use his name for a single – Nag, Nag, Nag – and they had suggested the possibility of our recording at their Western Works studio in Sheffield. We spoke with Chris after he came offstage, and gave him our honest appraisal of their performance when he solicited it. In that case, you won't be wanting to use Western Works, he snapped and ended our exchange.

TG came on dressed in white t shirts and white trousers, to a backing tape of the Village People's YMCA, Genesis striking pop star/dance poses in ultraviolet lights as the music gradually distorted, and became TG's. Again they were disturbing, aurally exciting and full of good humour. Some of their songs were surprisingly catchy, and we were singing – oh what a day, what a dull old day – on the way home.

Two days later and Nag and I were back in the same venue to hear the Red Crayola and Scritti Politti being supported by the Good Missionaries and The Transmitters. Mark Perry, the leader of the Good Missionaries looked a mess. He had shaved his own head, missing tufts of hair but cutting his scalp in others. He seemed distressed in performance as well, and ended by trying to smash his guitar up. It was more an act of despair than of any kind of rock guitarist catharsis. Later in the evening we collared him, asked him if he was ok and could we interview him for Common Knowledge?

The headline act were a sort of punk supergroup. The leader Mayo Thompson was the only original member of what had been an American band in the 60's, contemporaries of the 13th Floor Elevators. He had recruited Gina Birch from the Raincoats on bass, Epic Soundtracks from the Swell Maps as a drummer and Lora Logic playing sax, somehow a surprisingly tight combination.

Alison

Back in 1974 a free festival in Royal Windsor Park had ended in a messy protracted eviction, with long running skirmishes between the police and the "hippies", all within sight of one of the Queen's castles and broadcast on national TV.

The following year, in an attempt to pre-empt any similar event, an alternative venue was offered to the festival organisers – perhaps the only occasion when the State has provided a site for a free festival. The venue offered was an old Airforce base at Watchfield, a few miles outside of Swindon. I had managed to get my parents to drive me there most days which is how I came to spend 8 or 9 days there at the age of fifteen. My parents would pick me up again late in the evening, not allowing me to camp there overnight. Some days I went there with my brother (not yet called Snotcher!) but mostly I went with my girlfriend Alison. We had wandered around soaking up the music and getting a bigger exposure to the counterculture than Swindon – with its one band visiting every now and then - could usually provide. We naively strolled around, hand in hand fully clothed - amongst an audience that seemed to be mostly naked.

Alison would get very depressed if she drank alcohol and I couldn't cope with her low moods so after a few months I had retreated from our romance, but we had stayed friends. I admired her forthright honesty and feistiness. Alone amongst my friends she would stick to her principles, seemingly fearless of the teachers that the rest of us backed down to. We both started to study "A" levels at school but she declared that there was no point. She wanted to leave and start properly living her life. We saw less of each other and eventually she moved away to Bristol.

Now, suddenly, Alison turned up on our doorstep. I'd had no contact with her for a while and didn't know what she had been up to. She told us her story: She'd been living with a boyfriend but having been caught stealing a handbag and having also fiddled some dole money, she had been given a custodial sentence in some sort of borstal institution. Subsequently she had come to London rather than return to where she had been living in Bristol. She said that her old boyfriend was heavily into drugs and she didn't want to return to that scene.

My teenage hormones had had me relentlessly and fruitlessly searching for sex ever since I'd arrived in London, so I invited Alison into our house and into my bed. She said that she was happy to share my bed but that sex wasn't on the cards. She said that she had issues she needed to work out before she would be able to go there, so awkwardly we shared my bed for a few days. Then Igor rescued her and me by offering to pay the deposit for her on a local cheap bedsit. She moved in, saying that she was keen to spend some time on her own, wanting to work out what next to do with her life. I was humbled by Igor's generosity in sharing some of the small amount of savings that he had in the bank with an almost stranger.

Tufnell Park Mob

There was a small ad in Time Out every week offering casual work delivering leaflets. Just turn up at 8.30 on any weekday at an address in West Hampstead – just up the road from the Moonlight Club. We went there several times. Sometimes we were pissed off because they had enough people for the day already, but several times we got work. One day Igor, Nag and myself were surplus to requirements, along with a group of teenage girls. We got chatting to the girls, and got on with them. Several of them were in a band called Sherry Flips. They invited us to a party the following weekend. All of the friends said they lived in Tufnell Park, and they instantly became known to us as the Tufnell Park Mob.

The party to which they invited us seemed initially rather flat. Igor, Nag and I wanted parties to be a chance to meet exciting strangers and to share inspirations, to dance and to flirt. But this seemed to be a sit around quietly and pass the joint kind of party. I hated the influence of cannabis on parties – people konking out into private little reveries rather than coming together in communal celebration. Sitting on the floor with the others in a vague circle I was a little worried by the presence of a young skinhead sitting opposite me. I identified his haircut with a particular political view and with a threat of violence. He smiled and threw something at me. Something small. He threw a similar small thing at Nag, who was next to me. They were small blue tablets – Blues – said Nag – speed – eat it. So I did as instructed, offering a smile back to the donor. We got talking. He had short hair but was no skinhead. Fuelled with a couple more blues we spent the evening chatting. His name was Fritz and he was a drummer. He played in a band called 23 Skidoo. We liked him lots and Nag and I invited him to drum with us at our next gig at a pub called the Pegasus. When we got home I found that I had chewed away the inside of my cheek.

We'd invited Fritz round to visit, and a few days after the party he turned up – with seven of the Tufnell Park Mob! We all sat around in Nag's room – on the setee and on his bed and on the floor. We talked to the girls about their band Sherry Flips. During an evening of listening to records and drinking Pils lager I ended up snuggled up with one of the girls called Nicola. And it was the beginning of a relationship between Nag and the Flips' drummer Else. Fritz shared our enthusiasm for the newly released Metal Box by Public Image Ltd, but the girls' music tastes were more mainstream than ours. They were excited about the recent chart success of a ska band they knew from Camden, called Madness. The Special AKA single had recently come out and Igor had gotten a day's temporary work at Rough Trade, stamping the details onto the plain white sleeve, when the record had suddenly sold many more than expected. Apart from this single we had little in the way of the ska about which they were enthusing, but we found common ground in the African Dub series of albums put out by Joe Gibbs.

Crass

The anarchist punk band Crass were everywhere. Well, they were everywhere on the Central Line. They seemed to have stencilled graffiti onto the walls of every Central Line tube station from Essex to Ealing. Little brief slogans like *fight war not wars*, all signed with their logo. Nag had their 12 inch single *The Feeding of the 5000*, and although both of us found its lowest common denominator punk thrash a bit unlistenable, we were inspired by the words and the commitment and the politics. Igor thought their politics a little naïve, but it provided a starting point for lots of discussions. Live, Nag and I did a very slow version of their song *Do They Owe Us a Living?* with me putting on a posh vicar's voice.

I'd only just started going out with Nicola when we went to see Crass together. I called round at her housed to pick her up and as we left she'd shouted – bye Mum, bye Dad – I'm off out with Bendle – I'll see you tomorrow. I was amazed that although she was nearly a couple of years younger than me that her parents seemed unconcerned about her staying the night at my house.

Crass were playing at the Conway Hall, supported by two other anarchist bands: the Poison Girls and a group I'd not heard of before, the Rondos. We arrived at the central London venue and wandered in. There was a great atmosphere, all very peace and love. It reminded me of being at the Watchfield Free Festival despite most of the attendees being dressed in black leather jackets and sporting punk haircuts. Then at some point the atmosphere changed. Upstairs there was a balcony where someone had opened the fire exit, to let in a stream of skinheads. They circled around the balcony, spraying NF symbols on the wall. Open heartedness changed to fear and tension. The skinheads did nothing, but stood on the balcony exuding menace. I found it hard to concentrate on the Poison Girls' music, wary of the potential violence in the air. The support acts did their bits and then Crass took the stage. The moment they started to play the air was filled with flying bottles and the skins started to attack people. Nicola and I ran, out through the foyer and into the street – where there was more trouble and fighting - so we just kept running, until we got to the tube station.

Back at home Crass were inspiring us with their policy on record prices. They had put out a single called Reality Asylum with a price of 45p – about half of the usual cost of a single. We couldn't afford to price ours that low, but had decided to sell our second single for 55p.

Bobo had been true to his promise and had delivered his Revox to our house. For this record we had selected a mixture of pieces that we had recorded together and a couple of things that we had done separately. I'd written a song called *He Feels Like a Doris*, and had played Igor's organ and guitar. Nag had worked on his own on a track called Dig. We both played guitar on Nag's song *I Like Sound* with its bonkers lyrics – I like sound, I like noise, I like animals, I like toys... It was a long list of things Nag liked followed by a list of things he hated. We utilised the sound of an old spin dryer on my song *Production Line*.

We'd got our first single manufactured by a pressing plant called Orlake. We were a small unimportant customer to them and they had treated us badly. This time we approached Rough Trade and asked if they would get it pressed for us, hoping that they would have slightly more clout with the production plant. They were enthusiastic about what we were doing and suggested that they do a manufacturing and distribution (M&D) deal: they would pay for all the mastering and manufacturing costs and in return they would take enough copies of the record for distribution to recoup their costs. They suggested that we get 2000 copies of this single pressed.

Style and Influences

Igor came home with the Slits album. We were all impressed with the cover of three mud-smeared topless women and took it as a statement of female power rather than of titillation. And then the record. Because they had been in the audience at the early punk gigs, Nag and Igor knew most of the songs from time back way back. I knew them from the John Peel session in 1977 – but listen what they've done – Igor was keen to point it out before we said it – they've ditched any attempt at rock music, and based everything on reggae. We listened and analysed and listened again, tweezing out little sonic details – was that a matchbox used as percussion on the beginning of *Newtown*? Certainly there was the sound of a match striking a box. I taped the album straight away so that I could re-listen later in my bedroom.

Igor had brought home a book, too – *Subculture, the Meaning of Style*, by someone called Dick Hebdidge. Igor was the most intellectual of the three of us and was reading various left wing philosophers and theorists, books from the basement of Compendium. I was reading lots, but some of Igor's reading was over my head. I scanned the new book, about the ping-pong between black and white subcultures – it seemed more accessible.

I'd discovered Housman's Bookshop in King's Cross which had a huge wall of books just about Gandhi and was reading their anarchist magazines and booklets. Compendium Books in Camden was more cosmopolitan, with lots of stuff on music and art as well as politics. Nag and I often spotted a guy in Camden High Street whom we called The Tree Worshipper. An old tramp, he acquired his name from his habit of wobbling his head from side to side whilst staring at trees. The staff would put a chair out for him in Compendium and he'd spend Thursday mornings in there reading for free. Nag would pay attention to tramps and if they asked for money would always give them some. He said he might end up in the same state himself.

Several years ahead of me in their reading, Nag and Igor would direct me to books on their shelves. I was working my way through some modern classics and lots of stuff published by Picador. In my teens I'd been inspired by Tom Wolfe's *Electric Kool Aid*

Acid Test about Ken Kesey and the Merry Pranksters' experiences in the 60's. Now I explored how the acid had affected Kesey's consciousness by reading his *Sometimes a Great Notion*. When I moaned about Burrough's *Junky* being boring Nag had encouraged me to finish it by lying that it had a great twist at the end. He also introduced me to the rather lighter tones of Richard Brautigan and Kurt Vonnegut. Now he was urging me to read a biography of Stalin. It was a big book and at some point I ran out of energy. Feeling uninspired I retired to my room to blast myself with several different sound sources at once – un-tuned radios, cassette tapes and my reel to reel. This was becoming a reliable way to initiate ideas. I turned everything off and left the house, returning with a pile of second hand National Geographic magazines. I spent the rest of the day cutting them up and creating a collage covering the whole of one of the kitchen walls.

The local charity shops and junk shops in Crouch End provided objects to use as instruments and cheap clothes. My jeans were wearing out, but wearable, knees patched with gaffer tape, but I needed better shoes. I paid a visit to one of the grotty charity shops and left my old shoes behind, helping myself to a slightly better pair. I was lacking in any sense of style, apart from my NATO jacket. I'd designed a logo for TDATW and painted it on the back of my jacket in fluorescent colours, no words – I wanted it to be enigmatic. Mostly my clothes were dull, nondescript. If I was feeling flamboyant I'd wear an old white lab coat on which I'd painted a series of imperatives: Inspire; Organise; Create; Improvise, on top of flecks of multi-coloured paint.

Igor and Nag had known each other since school, and shared their own idiosyncratic language. I'd slipped into their world and understood that if one of them said "Morning, Glory", that the reply was "Evening, Standard!" Mostly I felt inside some sort of bubble with them, but occasionally would feel excluded from their banter, and wondered if this was how other people could feel around us if we were peppering our language with in-joke nonsense. Could it be that my flatmates, one so clever and one so seemingly confident, were feeling as insecure as me? I loved the lines from a song on the second Talking Heads album: *I have found a line and its direction is known to me, absolute trust keeps me going in the right direction.* Sometimes this was how I felt – I was following the thread and doing what was right for me to be doing, but much of the time I felt fearful in following this undefined path. Physically I had grown quite a bit in the last year, but internally still felt like the smallest boy in the class at school. There was a fearful voice inside of me that said: stop making yourself so visible.

Bad Music

Things were hotting up for the band. Our second single was being manufactured and we had a run of gigs. Fritz did the gig with us at the Pegasus, and unlike Grevious, he knew how to play the drums. We'd been to see his band rehearse in the room below Honky Tonk records shop in Kentish Town and had been unimpressed with the very average rock band noise they were producing. Fritz accepted our honest feedback with a smile, as did the guitarist Sam, who also became a friend. When they noted how impressed I was with the huge echo machine that they had in the rehearsal room they asked – did I want to borrow it? They weren't using it, I could have it for a while. And so I had a new sound to play with on my guitar.

We played a gig at the LMC where we showed the film that we had made with Giblet – we'd worked out several pieces of music to accompany it. The film caught in the projector and snapped, and we extended the music to go with it - but we were working with a backing tape and that ran out. I had to rewind the tape but to do so had to stop playing the guitar. To cope with his stage fright Nag had gotten drunk and was playing his parts wrong. It all felt like an embarrassing nightmare, but somehow we got applause from an audience of forty-odd people.

A couple of days later we were playing at the Bad Music Festival. Entrance was by donation and for both nights of the festival there was a decent sized crowd in the smallish venue. We got to meet Protag because the Instant Automatons had come all the way to London to play, and a band called Danny and the Dressmakers had come from Manchester. The Dressmakers were brilliant – performing inside of stretchy white semi-see-through bags (guitars and all), making a complete racket with humorous words. They implored Mr Rickenbacker to stop making guitars, and they sang the praises of Vimto. Both Protag and his fellow Automaton, Mark seemed warm hearted boys who had a great sense of humour. Kif Kif came onto the stage and held up a five pound note that someone had donated as their entrance fee. He made some sort of nonsensical statement about not needing money and burnt it. People cheered. Protag and I were confused. There was a band called The Hearing Aids playing, who had a tape out on Fuck Off with the great title: *All I Can Hear is the*

Sound of People Talking.

Bendle, Else (behind Kif Kif's drum kit), Nag,
Picture Mark Lancaster

We played with Else drumming (on Kif Kif's kit). She had bleached some of her hair and then hennaed it, and the result was a brilliant electric orange colour. Whereas Fritz had tuned into our songs and instantly managed to fit in with what we were doing, Else was a little nervous and unsure of what we were up to. Her way of compensating was to whack out some groovy beats and we had to try to keep up with her. It improved what we were doing! Our songs got faster. *He Feels Like A Doris* stopped being a dirge and got exciting. My guitar sounded great with the echo on it.

Else & Nag Acklam Hall Photo Mark Lancaster

Were we bad music? Good music at a bad music festival? Some of the acts were unmemorable or unmentionable, but we enjoyed the Automatons, and made a good connection with the two of them: Mark and Protag. Having used amps and drums that were in the venue we made our way home on the tube, the three of us and Nicola.

Mushrooms

Dance music came creeping into the house. Igor shared his love for the new Michael Jackson album (*Off The Wall*), and Fritz introduced me to the music of Funkadelic and Parliament. As much as I loved the industrial noise of Throbbing Gristle, or the absolutely abrasive sounds of Teenage Jesus and the Jerks and DNA on the *No New York* album, I had to reluctantly admit that there were pop sounds that also appealed to me.

We had no television, and no interest in owning one. For me news came into the house via the radio. At night we'd listen to John Peel. In the mornings my radio was tuned either to Radio 4 or to the local London news station LBC. I enjoyed the phone in programme hosted by Brian Hayes who seemed refreshingly intelligent (and somewhat arrogant). He would encourage informed debate but would often pull people's unthinking arguments to pieces or terminate their calls after labelling them as brainless bigots.

I went to visit my parents just before my student railcard ran out, and returned on the train with my bike. I cycled home from Paddington following the number 27 and 41 bus routes, but quickly began to learn my way around London without sticking to bus or tube routes.

We released our first album – on cassette. It was a mixture of live recordings; out-takes from the first single sessions and things that we had recorded at home on cassette. It included my machine-like *Reduction* produced by running Steve's drum machine through loads of effects pedals. Entitled *Permanent Transience*, our idea was that we would keep changing the cassette, in terms of covers, labels and content. The hard thing was finding a new piece of music to precisely fill the gap made by removing a track. We would end up having to record little snippets to fill in the gaps.

Initially we photocopied covers and labels and stuck the latter onto the cassettes with pritt glue. We started off copying them one at a time at home, but as we got more orders searched out somewhere we could get them copied. Kif Kif directed us to the man who had duplicated his Fuck Off Records releases, a jolly bearded guy called Flambo Yant. Flambo, who occupied a dusty room at Better Badges on Portobello Road, would copy us ten cassettes at a time, until we tired of changing the tape's content and just left a master with him. He sold some for us and gave us a reduced price on copying more. Flambo was a great fan of early Studio One reggae and compiled tapes for me of old singles from the label. I made him very happy by giving him a rare Lee Perry disc I'd found in jumble sale.

It was autumn and I was looking for mushrooms. I'd not picked Psilocybes before and wasn't quite sure what I was after. I'd cycle to different London parks and pick small mushrooms and then present them to Nicola and Else who were more experienced in these matters. Eventually with these two as guides we found some near their homes, on Parliament Hill. My secret hope in taking mushrooms was for spiritual illumination or some sort of enhanced psychic ability, but I was too embarrassed to voice this. I did however suggest that we indulge in serious psychological experiments, and Nag and Igor were willing to indulge me in this. With Else and Nicola we logged our initial explorations: 7.30 took 30 mushrooms; 8.00 mild nausea; 8.15 noticing electric red and green lines around the edges of people and of objects, feel giggly; 8.40 (in scrawled big letters) this is the most beautiful writing... and then nothing else.

Our giggly experiments led to enhanced pleasurable listening to music and, for me at least, an awareness of everything being connected to everything else. So maybe that was my spiritual illumination: experiential ecology, I named it in my diary. We repeated our attempts at logging our psychedelic trips but, without a non-participating observer, they were doomed to failure.

All three of us who were new to this experience decided it was the most healthy of druggy pursuits – up early in the morning, walking on Hampstead Heath or at Ally Pally to collect the mushrooms, and feeling the next day like the world had been polished, bright and fresh. Igor and I spent the whole of one trippy evening analysing the collage that I had made in the kitchen.

I went to visit friends in Matlock – not from the college, but the locals I'd met from the town. I spent a weekend there and then hitched back. Having been dropped by one lift near Alfreton, I explored a little shop that was selling off items cheap, and bought several packets of dried culinary herbs. On the sliproad of the M1 I was stopped by two policemen, and searched. A cook are we? They asked upon finding the marjoram and the thyme. Only in an amateur capacity, I replied in my most polite voice. And what about these? They'd found my little packet of dried mushrooms picked that weekend in the Derbyshire countryside. They are mushrooms, I explained – small but strong flavoured – Psilocybe semilanceata – I risked the proper name feeling too stressed to improvise another. Seemingly impressed by my sycophantic tones and my Latin terms, they let me go. I immediately stuck my thumb out, hoping earnestly for a lift to whisk me away before they returned.

Back at home we were excited when Green from Scritti Politti phoned us up inviting us to play on the bill of a Rock Against Racism gig with them at the Notre Dame Hall in Leicester Square. Affiliated with the AntiNazi League, Rock Against Racism had been promoting gigs ever since 1976 and we felt honoured to be on one of their billings.

We played a benefit gig at Finsbury Library Hall for Rock Against Blood Sports with Else drumming again – utilising the headline act's drum kit. They were a heavy metal band with a vast array of toms and cymbals, most of them unneeded by Else. We enjoyed playing, and an audience of friends and supporters enjoyed us. They kept shouting for more encores, until the promoter came on stage and pleaded with them to stop so that the next band could play. Our second single was out, and even got a joint "single of the week" review in Melody Maker – along with Ian Dury! We sold 900 copies in three weeks.

With dozens of artists putting out their own music, and actually managing to sell their records, it felt like the beginning of the end for the big commercial record labels. With Common Knowledge, we were trying to map what was happening, socially and politically. I was daunted by doing the interviews for the magazine, and asked fewer questions than my co-editors. Mayo Thompson of the Red Crayola had an intellect that scared Nag too, and we looked on bemused as he and Igor talked a slightly alien language. Nag and I conducted the interview with Mark Perry. I was nervous beforehand, meeting one of my heroes, but Mark was easy to talk to. At the end of the interview we enthused about his drumming on the last Alternative TV single, *Lost in Room*. We asked him if he would he be up for drumming with us at the Notre Dame Hall? We were amazed when he said yes, and bounced home full of excitement.

Kif Kif phoned us up. Would we like to do a free tour? He'd organised one before with (hippy band) Here and Now and Alternative TV, he could borrow Here and Now's bus. He suggested a billing including his band the 012 and the Sell Outs and Danny and the Dressmakers and the Instant Automatons. And The Door and the Window. We said we'd call round to discuss it. Igor told us not to – that we'd be associated with

West London Hippies, everything was going so well for us, but that we needed to be clear what image we were projecting...

Hippies

We walked the wrong way from Ladbroke Grove (that is, in the opposite direction to Rough Trade) to call round on Kif Kif. He lived in a tabloid cliché of a squat, with a co-collaborator in Fuck Off Records – introduced to us as JB. To get to where they lived, in the area known as Freestonia, we had to pass by some grim tower blocks and some interesting shops. These were officially lock up garages that had been converted into stalls selling fruit and veg and groceries run by and serving the local, mainly West Indian, population.

At Kif Kif's, JB was lying on the floor reading marvel comics, and seemed unembarrassed to be doing so. Kif Kif was trying to heat the place with a gas cooker that was running on full – we're running the meter backwards, he explained. He made Nag a cup of tea and furnished me with a glass of water and told us his plans, man. How about an EP to accompany the tour? One track from each band? Could we pay for our share of it? Well, we were quickly getting our money back from the second single, and so far it seemed that we could sell records with our name on. It seemed like a low risk enterprise so yes, we would record a track for the EP. Kif Kif showed us a picture that he thought would be good on the cover, a drawing of two clowns standing in the corner of a room, pointing out at and laughing – at us. We weren't as enthusiastic as him, but ok... His idea was to purchase some cheap plain white sleeves and to get the picture printed onto them at Better Badges.

November: In the world at large Lord Mountbatten was assassinated by the IRA. Closer to home Alison got arrested. It transpired that she had escaped from the borstal rather than having finished her time there. She had spent little time with us, believing that we were "just taking pity on her". Her arrest came about because she had had contact with her druggy ex-boyfriend, and he had informed the police of her location. I received a letter from her, telling me that she was to serve a custodial sentence in Holloway Prison.

Travelling around London with Nag, he would suddenly say something like – well, possibly. I'd ask- possibly what? And he'd get angry with me. He was having conversations in his head which at some point would become external. I was confused, but he was convinced that we'd been conversing and that I was just being awkward, pretending not to know what he was on about. One day at home he exploded, saying I was consciously planning to make him feel as though he was going mad. He was extremely upset and angry, and I was scared because he was shouting at me whilst holding a bread knife in one hand. Later when he was more calm, we talked this over. He had been doing the same thing, albeit less frequently, with Igor. He agreed to visit the doctor to ask about it. He was aware that he had also been sleepwalking, and had been found in the corridor one night by the tenant of the maisonette upstairs.

Igor and Simon had put out their Take It single – a three track EP properly recorded at a proper studio. In response to criticisms of it from Scritti Politti, Igor wanted to change direction with what they were doing. Discussion and disagreements about this led to Simon leaving, and Igor trying to work out what he would do next.

Nag and I went to meet Scritti ourselves – or at least the singer, Green, to chat about our forthcoming RAR gig. We met with Green in a pub in Camden, where he was just finishing an interview with an Australian woman called Vicky. Hearing her accent, Nag asked – do you know Bruce Milne? Bruce was an Australian radio DJ with whom Nag had been corresponding, the only person on that continent whose name he knew. Of course, said Vicky, and we began to chat with her as well as with Green. In the course of our conversation when I derogatively referred to someone as "a cunt", Green stopped me and pointed out the sexist nature of my language. Prick – he said, why not use that epithet, and explained why. Then he grilled me as to why in my song *He Feels Like A Doris* had I used a woman's name? Why not, perhaps, *She feels like a Horace*? I was a little flummoxed. My reading of Nag's Mum's Spare Rib magazines had made me consider my actions and interactions with women. They hadn't prompted me to consider my spoken language. Green was good humoured and very clever. I could see why Igor liked him. As he ran rings around me intellectually I said – you should be a lawyer. He replied that he was considering that option. Playing beat music was a temporary occupation. Vicky said she'd like to see more of us and invited Nag and I around for a meal the following week at her place.

There was a party the following weekend at Etta's house. Etta was one of the Tufnell Park Mob. She was an accomplished singer of old standards (that were unknown by me) like Summertime. Perhaps this group of friends should have been called the Dartmouth Park Mob – since they all lived in the rather more upmarket Dartmouth Park area adjacent to Tufnell Park. Each time we visited one of their houses it seemed more posh than the last. I'd not really thought about class before, but after visiting Nag's parents for a meal with Else, she had said to me that you could tell that they were working class – by the crap art on the walls. I had considered their furnishings and choice of art to be rather cosmopolitan and upmarket compared to my parents' home, so was initially surprised by her assertion. Else's words sound mean written down, but they were voiced it in a neutral non-judgemental way.

I had just previously spoken with Nicola and said that I wanted to end our relationship. I'd been prevaricating about saying it, but our spending time together didn't seem to be leading to a deeper level of contact. She was upset by the news. At the party Etta physically attacked me. How dare I treat her friend so badly? She ran at me, punching me in the face, and pushing me to the floor. A ring she was wearing chipped a little bit off of one of my teeth. I was shocked by her violence, and confused. It wasn't as though I'd ditched Nicola in favour of anyone else – I just didn't think it was working, and I'd bothered to say it honestly. Etta calmed down, and I stayed at the party.

It was getting late in the year but we were still finding a few magic mushrooms. Nag and I and Psi were collecting some in Kensington Park Gardens, putting our collection into a discarded plastic cup. I spotted a Parks Police vehicle approaching us. We put down the cup and drifted a few feet away from it. Questioned by the police, who had seen us scanning the grass we admitted that we had been looking for mushrooms, but no, not magic ones, we were looking for tomorrow's breakfast. They asserted that they knew what we were up to and that it was well known that although mushrooms were legal, that the people who take them also take cocaine and other illegal drugs. We were to leave the park now, and if we returned they would have our homes searched for illicit substances. We duly left the park, but quickly ran back to retrieve our cup of mushrooms when they had gone.

Nag and I had a rehearsal with Mark Perry, at Chris' place in Stroud Green – which was walking distance from our house. Chris was living in a large short life community house, with a number of other people. He had suggested that they all pool their incomes and live on equal amounts of money. No one else in the house had agreed – despite the fact that Chris was earning the most money. He had converted the cellar into a rehearsal space, complete with his drum kit and some of Psi's amplifiers and speakers. We could rehearse there for a meagre contribution towards electricity bills. Nag and I were nervous – this was the first time that we had actually rehearsed TDATW songs with anyone else, but Mark was positive about whatever we did. We all joked and laughed a lot, and working together was easy.

Mark caught the train South and Nag and I walked home. On the way Nag and I decided to call in on Thomas Leer again. The door was answered by a young woman called Madelaine, who had moved in. Leer had moved away. Would we like to come in? She had recently moved to London for work, but didn't feel drawn to socialising with her workmates. She knew no-one in London and was lonely. She offered us tea and biscuits and invited us to call back some time. I reflected on how different her experience of London was to mine. For me, London had rapidly become a playground. There was a chance of me running into people I knew – at gigs, in record shops or just in the street, not just in Hornsey, but all across London.

Igor formed a new band, with the same name. A friend of Nag's called Jim would play slap bass, Else was the drummer and a guy called Nic would play guitar. Igor would sing and play violin. Initial rehearsals were at our house, but they quickly moved on to using the same space as 23 Skidoo - below Honky Tonk Records in Kentish Town.

Weird Noise

Come the night of the Notre Dame Hall gig there was dispute over the running order of the bands. The posters said: Essential Logic, Scritti Politti, The Door and the Window, Delta 5 (Admission charge £1.80). The Delta 5 had come down from Leeds with the impression that they were higher up the bill, and were selling lots of copies of their Mind Your Own Business single. We had no interest in arguing and agreed to go on first.

As we took the stage, an organiser for Rock against Racism asked me if I would announce that it was one of their gigs and welcome people. I did as he said, and in horror heard my voice coming through the PA in an echo of his Jamaican accent. I brought my voice back to normal, and wanted to hide, but Mark was hitting the drums. We responded well to the large venue, and worked well as a trio. We ended with a version of Production Line (from the second EP), augmented with the voices of Psi, Garry (who was in London visiting someone else) and his sister and a young bloke called Alan Tyler. The audience was enthusiastic. Afterwards Vicky (who had recorded the gig for us on cassette) was raving about my wonderful backwards Gary Glitter guitar sound, and Igor was consoling us about the billing order – You won't be bottom of any bill again after tonight.

The next day Nag suggested that we invite Mark to become a permanent member of the band. I had a fear of the word permanent, was worried that it would be the end of its being coupled with the word transience. Nag reassured me that in the same way that we had been a duo and sometimes had added an extra person, now we could be a trio and do the same. It was hard to argue with Nag and I agreed. We rang Mark up and he agreed to join the band.

Our next performance was not as TDATW. Vicky had invited Nag and I and her new flatmate Jim to be her backing band for a poetry reading at a small venue in West London. Jim was known to us as a guy who worked in the large HMV on Oxford Street, in which capacity he had bought some TDATW singles. We had no rehearsals, and Vicky just instructed us to make a horrible noise. We did as instructed. The other acts playing that evening seemed pretentious and boring – apart from Giblet who read a few poems. One group played interminable bad covers of Pink Floyd songs. We felt that we were doing a positive thing by stealing their wah wah pedal for my use rather than theirs. Afterwards we went back to Vicky's place.

When she had invited us round to dinner Vicky had been living in North London. Now she was living in a new flat in Notting Hill. A whole block of brand new flats had been squatted. She was living with Jim and a guy called Keith Allen. Jim Thirlwell was originally from Australia and Vicky knew him from Melbourne. Keith was known to us as someone who worked for X3 printers – they did amazing fluorescent posters for bands. He was also in a band called the Atoms and was doing some comedy. He was sleeping on what looked like a dentist's chair. Else came back with us, and all four of us managed to squeeze into Vicky's bed, though we didn't get much sleep through lack of space and Vicky's loud snoring.

At the end of November I went on an anti-Tory government march from Hyde Park to Parliament, walking with Nag and some other friends. We politely ambled in a long moving queue and chanted as advised. We were demonstrating just how boring the opposition could be. None of us was impressed.

We had recorded a song for the Weird Noise EP – *The Number One Entertainer* – Nag singing away like a strangely drugged working men's club singer, with my very basic guitar line underneath it. The other groups' songs were ready to go. We particularly liked the 5 short contributions from Danny and the Dressmakers, and were disappointed when Kif Kif said that they wouldn't be coming on the tour after all. One of them had a job and couldn't get off of work. This sounded crap to us, but Kif Kif thought it was more exemplary anti-rock and roll attitude. Oh, and they weren't going to pay their share of the costs, could we pay a bigger proportion?

And then with the next meeting or the next phone call – uh the Sell-Outs, man, they're having trouble raising their contribution for the EP, uh we'll all have to pay a little more. And next of course Kif Kif himself was having money trouble. Sod it, NB Records would fund the whole bloody thing. We got it mastered – at Porky's again – cue more laughter, and arranged with Island to press it. It was only later that we found that they had subcontracted to Orlake, the plant that had treated us badly with our first single. They failed to have the EP ready for the tour.

The tour was scheduled for a number of dates around the middle of December. A few days before the first gig, Kif Kif phoned up. There was a problem with the bus, man, we couldn't use the Here And Now bus after all. I was completely despondent – well, that's it for the tour, I guess. No said Kif Kif, he'd work something out. My image of Kif Kif by this point was merging with that of the titular protagonist of William Kotzwinkle's *The Fan Man*, and I doubted whether anything would come of all this planning.

Then two days before the tour, Kif Kif phoned again. He'd bought a bus. He'd bought a bus? What kind of bus does a man with no money buy? It transpired that it was a decommissioned ambulance – the sort that they use to ferry around disabled or elderly people, not an emergency ambulance. We stacked it with speaker cabinets face down on the floor, with a drum kit and amps and leads squeezed in where we could, and then most of us sat on top of the equipment. Nag and Mark and myself, Kif Kif and JB, Protag from the Automatons (without Mark), Giblet, tagging along and Psi, who had loaned some of his PA. (Psi, in fact had now changed the spelling of his name to Cy). The brakes on the vehicle didn't work well – Kif Kif had to judge junctions so that we could just keep rolling along. If we did manage to stop, then we'd all have to jump out and give the thing a push.

So, shambolically, we rolled into High Wycombe to play at the Nag's Head. The "tour" had been reduced down to 4 nights. The 012 was Kif Kif singing and playing guitar, with a drummer picked each night from the audience. For the first night Giblet was their drummer. Kif Kif drummed with the Sell-Outs, with JB singing. The Automatons were listed on the ads, but were represented by just Protag, who was perhaps the most polished performer, with real rehearsed songs. For our part we did what we did. The whole thing seemed rather ludicrous and we managed to laugh at ourselves.

The second night we played somewhere called the Nowhere Club in Bicester. The audience seemed to be largely composed of young Americans with short hair. I felt rather intimidated by them, but fuelled with beer they cheered at all the acts. They were mostly men based at USAF Upper Heyford. At the end of the evening a group of them asked where we were sleeping. We didn't know. Did we want to come back to their place? They had rented a huge house and whilst they cooked up enough soup for everyone, they said that we could sleep in any empty room we chose – several of which had mattresses in them. So, feeling well fed and cared for, we had a comfortable night's sleep.

Next night we were back in London, playing at a pub called the Chippenham. A small room in a small pub – but one with musical history – the 101ers had played here. At some point Cy invited himself onstage on a second guitar, and then I realised that we had also been joined by Roddy Disorder of the Murphy's on trumpet and a mate of his on trombone. We'd become a big band! We were euphorically happy – and the audience seemed to be too! Afterwards Mark went home, Nag and I crashed at Kif

Kif's.

The vehicle wouldn't start the next day, no matter what we did with it. We were due to play in Bristol at the Trinity Hall. Don't worry, said Kif Kif, I know a Buddhist truck driver. The Buddhist was found, with his lorry, and was willing to drive us to Bristol. We unloaded the ambulance and loaded up the truck, and set off down the M4. Several hours later, unpacking the load at the venue, Protag asked where was the bread crate of leads he had put in the back of the truck? Someone had taken it out in order to pack more efficiently... they remembered putting it under the lorry. Kif Kif made a desperate phone call from a payphone to friends in London. Amazingly, the crate was lying where we had left it. Cy and Protag would have to try to bodge together a working PA from the bits and bobs we had.

The audience of about 50 looked lost in a reasonably large venue, but they were a fun crowd and the evening seemed to be a success for the few that made it there. People put enough in the proverbial hat to pay for the petrol. Tour over, we all drove back to London, rather tired. The effect of fatigue on Nag seemed to be that he spoke more crap. He'd been to see our useless local doctor, who said that he would refer him on for an appointment with a specialist, but that hadn't happened yet.

Christmas

After the tour I caught the coach to Swindon and stayed with my parents and my brother for a few days for Christmas, then travelled back to London. My parents were concerned – had I found a job yet? No, but I was sure that I would soon. And actually, for once I was being honest – I was looking for some way of bringing in a little money.

In Swindon I went to the pub where I knew old schoolfriends would be hanging out. Jim, the least trendy and most straight forward of my friends had moved away. I felt no connection with any of the people who were home from university for Christmas, and left the pub early. On subsequent visits to Swindon to visit my parents, I made little effort to socialise with my old school mates, preferring to spend time my brother and his new friends.

We had planned to spend New Year with Vicky. She and I had begun an informal affair. We never thought of each other as boy/girlfriend, but every now and again one of us would phone the other and ask if they wanted to spend the night together. It felt like a very easy uncomplicated relationship. Vicky was working in temporary office jobs in the daytime and out listening to bands in the evenings. She was a large jolly presence speeding her way through her days in London.

Nicky Sudden from The Swell Maps had moved into a tiny room in the flat. It was meant to be a store room, but just about housed a single mattress. He was elsewhere for New Year, as was Jim. Keith had bought a saxophone a week or so before, an instrument that he couldn't play, but was determined that he was going to play tunes on it through the streets on New Year's Eve. He had apparently been practising with it since Christmas, and on New Year did as he had said he would, and set off to play to people walking to or from parties. Nag and Else and Vicky and I went to a reggae do up the road at the Tabernacle. I lost the others and stayed up all night with a couple of young punk girls who lived nearby. I wandered back to Vicky's for breakfast the next morning passing the Spanner Tramp on the way. An old Jamaican, he was so named because of the necklace of spanners that he wore on top of his layers of coats and ponchos. He had so many layers that he appeared to be conical in shape. He was one of a number of memorable street people in Notting Hill including the woman who busked by playing a wind-up gramophone that she wheeled around in a pram, and an African man who would stand very still wearing tribal gear and brandishing a vertically pointing spear. The Spanner Tramp demanded that I buy him some bread and I found a shop that was open so that I could comply.

49 Americans

Giblet had said that he wanted to make a single. We said that we would put it out via NB records. He had been recording one or two tracks at a time on Igor's cassette recorder over December and we finished the EP in early January. Realising that a 45 rpm seven inch single could hold a maximum of seven minutes of music per side, he had decided that his EP would have seven tracks per side, each 58 seconds long. The band was called The 49 Americans, but different combinations of people were used on different songs. There were two tunes played by the Rickets – a setting to music of Newton's laws of motion and a heavy metal analysis of Heisenberg's Uncertainty Principle. I was proud of a mangled guitar sound that I produced over a background of clanking metal percussion for *Pigs*, one of the poems that Giblet had read on the tube after the Swell Maps gig. Else drummed on lots of the songs, but since they were recorded in our house and Giblet's parents, mostly utilised a kit composed of pots and pans and cardboard boxes. Igor sang and played on it, and Nag played his Wasp, and both he and I slapped our bellies as percussion. The single ended with a chorus of three mums – Nag's, Igor's and Giblet's singing *Stupid Boy*, with the last line: *He thinks he's made a record – stupid boy!* The only Americans on the record were Giblet, his Mum and his brother. I felt that it was full of profound ideas wrapped up in flippant humour!

For packaging we would use a similar method to the second TDATW single – a plain white cover enclosed in a sandwich of two pieces of coloured card held in a plastic sleeve. The plain white labels on the record would have stickers on them – USA side and USB side. Giblet drew a cover of line drawings of 49 little figures and we got a sticker printed for the cover announcing – Contains the hit album!

Early in January we took Giblet's music to be mastered at Porky's. His never-ending smile nearly got broken this time. Either we had failed to explain, or Giblet had failed to understand that he needed his tape edited into the correct order. Poor George had to not only master from a crappy cassette tape, but he had to edit it too. He added "E pluribus unum" to the A side runout groove and added – Porky. On the B side Giblet had requested "Anyone can be president". Usually the procedure was to leave a master with Porky and arrange for someone from a pressing plant to collect it. Today though, Giblet and Nag took the single to a pressing plant called Allied, and I went on to Island Records offices to collect the Weird Noise EP.

This was the first time I had been in the offices of a large record company, and I got to check the playing quality of the single in a plush lounge. It was rather incongruous, listening to Danny and the Dressmakers in such luxury. Having nodded my assent at the quality, a secretary arranged for a van driver to deliver both me and the singles back to our house.

Nag and I had collected the covers from Better Badges. We added the stickers to the blank white labels and inserted the records into the sleeves. We relieved the hours of tedium by scrawling labels on some of the records rather than adding stickers. Mostly we added insults to Kif Kif – there were "Kif Kif thinks this shit is a record" EPs, and "Kif Kif fucks like a rabbit" EPs. There were also some Weird Nose EPs. Some of the covers had got caught in the printing press which wasn't designed to print on already glued together pages, and they were either torn or creased or badly printed. If there was a fold where nothing had been printed we doodled it in. We boxed them up with the best covers showing at the tops of the piles, and were relieved to find that they sold quickly, and that we would regain the money that we had invested. They had completely sold out by the end of January.

Early in January also, Common Knowledge was ready to be printed. We had negotiated a deal with Joly at Better Badges, who as well as making badges, suddenly seemed to be printing all of the fanzines with large circulations. His proposal was that he would print a thousand copies of our A5 sized magazine, charge us nothing for doing so, but would keep and sell 800 copies. We would get 200 copies for free. Our plan was to sell a hundred copies ourselves to provide money for envelopes and stamps to give the other hundred away.

Orbit of Scritti

We found ourselves being drawn into the orbit of Scritti Politti. From their messy squat in Carol Street or from their nearest pub – dubbed The Bright Pub - the three members of the band held court to a large number of friends and allies who were planning on changing the world via their musical activity. Tom, the drummer, was the first white bloke I'd met with dreadlocks. He had scary piercing blue eyes, and I couldn't hold his gaze. Green was pretty and clever and charming, but my favourite in the band was Nial, the bass player, who seemed to be the most down to earth, and who undermined any earnestness on the part of his band mates with his smile and dry humour. They were good friends with an intellectual NME journalist called Ian Penman, who would sometimes join them on stage playing saxophone under the name of Peewee Pascal.

We were invited to join a number of bands who were going to put out a compilation album. Nag and I attended a meeting at the Bright Pub to discuss some of the ins and outs of what would happen. Mark had wisely declined attending the meeting, which we found rather tedious. Every idea was analysed for its motivations and dissected in terms of its political meaning. Nag and I quickly decided that there was a lot of talk happening, but not a lot else going on.

We made friends from that circuit of people, notably the members of bands called Reptile Ranch, The Puritan Guitars and The Janet and Johns. The latter were two boys from Cardiff called Charles and Hywell. They got us two gigs in Cardiff, and said they'd arrange drum kit and amps, so that we could travel there on the train. The three of us had a great weekend staying in a little house in Splott, and playing two small venues. Our hosts also somehow managed to summon up an audience. We went down well, and some of the people from the Friday night paid to come and see us again the next night. We had abandoned the reel to reel and were more flexible without it. Songs could be however long we wanted them to be, and it was easier to do two different sets two nights on the trot – since we were still committed to never playing the same set twice.

We returned home to London on the Sunday. Monday morning Nag and I lugged 300 copies of the Weird Noise EP to Rough Trade. In the afternoon Igor and I went to visit Alison in Holloway. We were both nervous going into the prison. It felt a little unreal, like walking into a film set, except when we got to the visitors' room, there was our friend, looking scrawny and edgy. We talked awkwardly in the gaze of the prison guards and passed her the cigarettes that we had brought her. We got her to suggest a list of books that we could get for her, and promised to visit again.

I saw January out walking a protest march against transportation of nuclear waste on the North London (railway) Line with Simon and his girlfriend Geraldine, which felt like a dull carrying out of duty. Fear of nuclear war or of a nuclear accident were always in the air. More positively, Nag and I celebrated that we completely sold out of the Weird Noise EP, and on the last day of the month I got a job.

I became a part time Handyman at an old people's home in Muswell Hill called Charles Clore House (which I referred to as CCH). For five mornings' work I would be paid £32. After deductions for tax etc I would take home £28. I somehow convinced the matron that I could do general maintenance chores, mend plumbing and do the gardening. I was given the key to the handyman's room in the basement where my tools were kept, and a notebook. Each day I would collect the book from the matron's office in the morning and work my way through the list of tasks that she had compiled for me.

Street Level Studio

Kif Kif had asked us for money again, only this time the deal was different. If we joined the Dirt Cheap Studio Club for £100 then we could have access to his studio at a discounted rate – when he had built it! Despite the debacle with the Weird Noise tour and EP we didn't dismiss the idea immediately. He was doing the studio with Grant Showbiz and a guy called José. Mark knew Grant as the man on the sound desk from a couple of tours, and liked him. There were other people putting money up front, maybe the studio would happen. We had invested £100 of NB Records money.

Suddenly it was hard to fit everything in. The 49 Americans' single was ready and needed packing, and Common Knowledge had been printed. Nag and I were interviewed for Melody Maker by Hannah Charlton, and the studio *did* happen so we booked in time to record an album, and I was trying to hold down a new job.

Mark declined to be part of the interview. We'd gotten more attention since he had joined the band, but if people asked him about his new project, he would say – I'm just the drummer – ask them. Partly it was modesty on his part, partly he was glad to be out of the limelight. Melody Maker had a flattering picture of the two of us, but the article was uninformative and not really very interesting. Melody Maker was the most dull of the three main weekly music papers. The NME was the best with some of the best writers, like Penman and Paul Morley. Sounds was less good, but had a couple of good writers including Jon Savage and Sandy Robertson who seemed interested in industrial noise and experimental music. Unimpressed with the MM article we were much happier with the positive 49 Americans' reviews in all of the papers – and even the negative ones seemed funny, and were good publicity.

Nag and I were also interviewed on Capital Radio. This turned out to be a lesson about the media and the power of the edit. We lurked in the control room listening in on the interview with the next guest, the reggae artist Mikey Dread. The DJ just wanted to ask Dread about "jamming with the Clash" on their UK tour. Dread wanted to talk about the political situation in Jamaica, and how baffled he was about the lack of reporting in the UK about how bad things were there. The interviewer just kept asking questions about music, which Dread would answer politely, briefly, and then try to return to discussing Jamaican problems. When we listened to the interview aired later that evening, all of the politics had been edited out, and all the musical discussion seamlessly edited together.

There were no political songs on the 49 Americans single but many assumed the name alluded to the American hostages held prisoner in the embassy in Iran. Originally there had been 52 of them, but at one point there had been 49 as the political impasse dragged on. We didn't let on that Giblet's inspiration for the name had been a song by Pere Ubu called *49 Guitars and One Girl.*

Kif Kif and Grant's studio had been built in a basement on a run down street in West London. It was a grotty building, but they had cleaned out the cellar and put in a recording room and a control room. It actually had decent microphones and speakers and amps, a one inch 8 track recorder and a quarter inch tape for mixing. There was a huge reverb plate in the corridor. The carpet didn't stink yet of beer. Grant was going to record us. He was an irresistible loudmouth. I'd had misgivings because I'd first noticed him on the mixing desk at a gig in Derby 15 months previously. Mark had been playing his experimental new music to the punks who wanted him to play Alternative TV's hits. Someone had thrown a bottle which hit Mark. Grant had shouted "more". Weird sense of humour.

The recording process was familiar to Mark, but alien to us, recording one or two parts at a time and overdubbing the next bit. It all seemed painfully slow, and Nag and I were watching the clock, fretting about the cost. We wanted to do a very different version of Subculture Fashion Slaves from the one on our first single. We recorded Mark and Nag's parts, and then I added an amazing guitar part. I even managed to keep playing when my guitar strap snapped. Brilliant, said Grant through the headphones... now can you do it again with the tape running?

I'd written a song about miscommunication between generations. Originally I had titled it *Nag's Dad*, because although not specifically about him, it was inspired by a conversation with him. I'd retitled it as *Dads* to make it more generic, but Mark kept trying to wind Nag up by referring to it as *Nags*.

> Record your independent single/album/cassette
>
> at **STREET LEVEL**
>
> ★ DISGUSTING TOILET!
> ★ HORRIBLE BACK YARD!
> ★ CRAZY ENGINEERS!
> ★ AIR-CONDITIONING!
> ★ 8 TRACK ONE INCH AMPEX!
> ★ FANTASTIC SOUND!
>
> "Simply the coolest Studio in town" (MARTIN ATKINS)
>
> special Fanzine Makers £6.50 p.hr. rate!
>
> :.7337 ☆ 289.9699

We'd record from early afternoon into the evening and then head home. If it seemed that we shouldn't stop we'd work into the night, and then sleep on the studio floor. We worked over the weekend, but at least once I went from the studio across London to work. Everything was recorded in a matter of days rather than weeks, but my sense of time was mangled. Grant cajoled us to re-record things until he felt that he had captured our best, and we were proud of what we had done. Recording parts of a song at a time freed us up a little. It meant that Mark could overdub saxophone parts on a couple of songs, and we swapped instruments around a little. I played drums on one track. Nag and I each played bass on one tune and we added a toy piano and a cheap organ to our instrumentation. Mark also sang on a couple of songs.

We delayed the mixing of the album for a little while so that we'd revisit it with fresh ears. Nag and I had done a little mixing with Bobo's Revox, but this was 8 tracks and more complicated. Mark was more of a veteran in terms of studio experience, and it was good to be working with him. Grant was tied up with other commitments so Kif Kif did the mixing with us. It ended up being a slightly protracted affair as some of the equipment kept malfunctioning, so we'd have to postpone and return another day.

I was tempering my experience of being in a recording studio with my new job in the old folks home. I would hop out of bed and, without breakfast, cycle up a backroad to the top of Muswell Hill, pausing part way up to buy a bar of chocolate to boost my low blood sugar. At work I'd collect my notebook and come up with a plan of what to tackle first. There would be sliding toilet doors that needed re-siting on their rails, loose fittings that needed tightening, bedroom sinks that needed unblocking. I quickly realised that the main reason resident's sinks were blocked was because people had tried to wash turds down the plughole. Cleaning shit out of a u-bend is about as much fun as it sounds.

My Dad has always been an expert at any kind of DIY, and although I had zero experience of doing anything useful around the house, I'd observed enough to bluff my way through things. If jobs looked too big and daunting I'd explain to the Matron that the task required tools that we didn't have and that she would have to employ professionals to do the job. Although our garden in Ferrestone Road had failed to produce a crop of vegetables, I was aware of which plants in the grounds of Charles Clore House needed tending, and which were considered weeds. My appreciation of plants didn't quite coincide with the matron's, however. One day there was an instruction in my notebook to prune the roses. Hating cultivated roses, I cut back all the domesticated bits and just left the suckers in the hope that they would revert to wild forms. I endured the subsequent admonishment and carried on as usual.

I shared my basement with a laundry run by an Italian man who I called Pokerville. He was forever telling me how wonderful a lover-man he was, and how popular he was with the ladies. I wondered if there were any truth to his boasting at all, and if there was, did his girlfriends know that he worked in a laundry in the basement of an OAP home? Also in the basement there was a mortuary room, that I felt no urge to investigate, and another room that I did. This was the room where dead residents' unwanted belongings were stored. Once people's relatives had taken away whatever keepsakes they wanted, the deceased's things were deposited ready for collection by a charity shop or a rummage sale organiser. I thought that since they were unwanted clothes that I could help myself. I found a pair of shoes for myself and began to look out for sizes to fit Nag and Igor.

Nag and I had recently visited Small Wonder, a small but influential East End record shop that ran its own record label, to sell copies of the Weird Noise EP. Pete, the owner, was a cynically humorous old hippy, and it was always fun to drop stuff off there. On this visit we ran into Colin, one of the Final Solution promoters, and he'd invited us to a party at his place.

At the party our hosts offered us lines of sulphate, which we eagerly accepted. Nag had been taking speed occasionally ever since his punk days and since Fritz had introduced me to blues I'd also tried speed in powder form. It was a treat for special evenings out when we could get hold of it. I'd heard lots of conspiracy theories as to why it was harder to get hold of than it had been. The story went that the powers that be thought that young punks on speed might actually try to change the world as they were threatening to. Better to sedate them. Suddenly it was easy to get hold of tuinal, a barbiturate. In the streets, at gigs and at parties I saw spiky haired punks doped into ugly stupidity. I wasn't sure about conspiracy theories, but did wonder about the route by which these pharmaceutical drugs ended up on the streets. Certainly I was not going to try a drug that turned you into a twerp. Cannabis used on its own was bad enough. We thought, that if you are going to take a drug that makes things seem more magical, or that gives you inspiration, then take another with it so that you actually use it to do something positive. Speed made cannabis positive. Failing speed, try caffeine!

The Pop Group were at the party. Nag was wary of them – he'd included the band amongst his list of hates on *I Like Sound*. They seemed like bigger than life characters to me and I started to talk to Mark, the singer. From a distance I thought that with his hat and jacket and red shirt he looked like a matador. He started talking about all the bad things in the world that from his political perspective needed changing, and then proceeded to lecture me on the ways in which magic was the solution to our problems. I couldn't really understand his train of thought, and he was getting into monologue mode, so I drifted away.

The next night Igor, Nag and I celebrated Giblet's birthday at his house with him and his family. We joined his Mum in the preparation of a Chinese meal. She was a kind host but a strict task master who wanted all the vegetables cut in precisely the right way. No, my ginger was not sliced finely enough! Giblet's Dad was a lecturer at the School of African and Asian Studies. Both of his parents used the name Giblet when we sang happy birthday to him. We'd taken literally something he had said about wanting to smash up a pumpkin with a mallet and as a birthday gift gave him these two items.

Mark

Mark had grown up in Deptford and that was where he was living again, now. After one of our rehearsals at Chris' place we went to visit his flat and to meet his flatmate. We got on the overground at Haringey station, heading south on the first stage of our journey. Across the aisle from us were three young black men. Suddenly one of them got up and forced open the sliding doors of the moving train and two of them grabbed me, forced me over to the open door and threatened to throw me out. We don't like white racists, they said. Mark got up to come to my rescue but was wary of them just pushing me out. We're not racists, he said, we're good socialists. Somehow he charmed them or calmed them down, and I was allowed to return to my seat. My assailants just laughed, as we hurriedly got off of the train at the next stop to board the tube.

Mark's flatmate, Bob, was a left wing political activist, and also a ventriloquist. His dummy was a life-sized model of himself! The flat they shared was a council property in a postwar four storey high tenement block. A section of the local overground railway curved round nearby on a viaduct, and at night it looked like the trains were going to drive in through the window. I'd thought that Mark, the bloke that started the biggest selling punk fanzine, friend of all the luminaries of that scene, would have a ground zero taste in music, rejecting all things pre-76. This was not the case. He introduced us to some of his current enthusiasms – the free jazz of the Art Ensemble of Chicago and beat rap of The Last Poets. Then he surprised me by pulling out a Simon and Garfunkel album. What? Wasn't that crap for our parents? No, he said, and played us Bookends. I wasn't convinced, but loved his eclectic taste and his passion. He lacked any kind of pretension.

From his involvement with Step Forward and Deptford Fun City Records, and from the sales of the Alternative TV recordings he was living on a small but regular weekly wage. On Fridays he would go to the offices of the parent company - Faulty Products - to collect his money. The offices were in Blenheim Crescent, not far from Rough Trade. Nag and I would meet him there on a Friday afternoon after I had finished my shift at CCH. Then we would go for something to eat in Mike's café – a greasy spoon place where we'd have something like liver and onions, and then often go on for a drink in the Blenheim Arms. Sometimes we'd meet up with Dennis Burns and another ex-bandmate of Mark's called Henry Badowski, who looked like he was about to become a pop star as a solo artist, having made a couple of catchy singles.

Faulty was run by an entrepreneur called Miles Copeland – who was also the manager of The Police. Mark had to reassure us about both Miles and the company. Prior to Mark joining the band Nag and I had decided we hated Faulty. They had taken some of our first single for distribution, but had been very reluctant to pay us later on. Whenever we called the receptionist said that unfortunately the accountant was out or that he was at a meeting. One time when we were there Nik Turner, the old hippy saxophonist who had played with Hawkwind turned up, likewise asking for money that he was owed. Our approach had been one of politely explaining our annoyance. Nik just threatened: Have the money tomorrow. If he's still pretending that he's not here I'll chop his fucking door down with an axe!

Step Forward had put out records by The Fall, and Mark introduced us to the band in a pub near to the offices. They were a friendly effusive bunch, all except for Mark Smith, who sat alone in the adjoining bar, and just asked for directions to the nearest chippie before vanishing.

Detailed Twang

We had decided to call the album Detailed Twang, after one of Nag's songs. I was trying to design the cover, and had decided that what I needed were bits of sheet music to cut up. I couldn't find the right material. I'd visited Simon and Cy in King's Cross and stayed the night in Godfrey's room – he never seemed to be there. I'd woken early and nosed at Godfrey's copies of *The Teachings of Don Juan* and *The Doors of Perception*, waiting for Simon to get up. Then I had breakfast and set off for home. Outside the flats were two large metal communal waste bins. I'd regularly check them out in the same way I'd look in skips for useful items. Today I found a heap of junior school music books. I rushed back to show Simon my find, and then set off for home again to show Nag.

The books contained the bits of sheet music that I had been looking for, but also some great explanatory text:

> they loved drumming and had a great sense of rhythm

and

> The tension becomes more and more frightening as the strange sounds unfold; the old story with all of its mystery and magic, comes alive.

Nag and I picked a selection of bits of text that made us laugh, and jumbled it all up with cut-ups of sheet music. For the back cover we wanted some photos. A guy called Ken Ansell lived nearby. He edited a magazine about improvised music called Impetus, and because of this we always referred to him as Old Impetus Features. We'd met him through the LMC and he had taken some pictures of us playing at the Rock against Racism gig. Because there were no good pictures of Mark, we asked him if he would come round and take a few more of us in our front/rehearsal room.

We took tapes of the album to play to Rough Trade (in a new office, round the corner from the shop), hoping for another M&D deal. We were invited to play the album to Mayo Thompson, who still seemed a slightly daunting figure to us. We were aware of his music with various line ups of the Red Crayola dating back to the 60's, and Igor was very keen on his album of political songs with Art and Language. Listening to our song *Sticks and Stones*:

> We've got to use our gumption, stick together not fall apart
> I want to go down in history as being present at the start

Mayo grilled us – Present at the start of what? His were reasonable challenges, but his questions felt like being interviewed for a job. Nag and I withered a little under his questioning, and guessed he was going to reject the album – but no, he smiled and said that they would manufacture it for us. We had to sort the printing of the sleeves and to get the recording mastered. Rough Trade would arrange collection of the master and subsequent manufacture of the records.

We took our cover art to a company in Soho Square for printing. On our way into the building we ran into Sleazy from Throbbing Gristle who was there in his role as one of the Hipgnosis designers. It felt like a good choice of printer if Hipgnosis were using them, since they worked for record companies with big budgets. The guy who met us looked with horror at our art work. Christ – what had we stuck pictures on with? Bluetack! He explained that the artwork had to pressed between layers of glass to be photographed and had to be flat. He provided a tin of cow gum and gave us half an hour to re-do the cover.

Nag had still been sometimes imagining conversations in his head. He also lied lots – his description of events seemed to me to be idealised versions of what he would have liked to have happened rather than what other people witnessed. Before I knew him he had fabricated the whole of an interview with the Ramones for the New Wave Magazine which was printed before he admitted what he had done. Despite this I felt him to be the most honest person that I knew. If he felt something, he would bluntly say it, and asked a question would give a straight answer. He was also stubborn – if he wanted something he'd hold out for it – negotiating things with him was not easy. The referral that his GP had promised him came through and he had an appointment with a psychologist. Nag reported that the consultant just said that he thought that he was an absent minded genius, and had discharged him with a bottle of Valium tablets to help him sleep.

The same day as his hospital appointment we played the first 49 Americans gig, at the LMC. This was a convoluted affair, with lots of people in the band, all seated in chairs in rows. For any particular song a combination of four or five people would stand up to perform. We each had a little chart to show who was playing and when and to whom they should pass on their instruments. Probably because there were quite a few of us in the band, and all of us had friends in the audience, we had a fair sized crowd to cheer us on.

Double Drums

From our having produced Common Knowledge Igor, Nag and I were invited to a forum of fanzine editors, where we met lots of people including Tony Fletcher from Jamming and Tony D from Kill Your Pet Puppy. For some reason the meeting was chaired by Robert Wyatt, whose name seemed to be suddenly everywhere. Scritti were enthusing about his music, and Igor had dug out his copies of *Rock Bottom* and *Ruth is Stranger than Richard*, and introduced me to those wonderful records. Most of the people at the meeting seemed to be getting their work printed at Better Badges, where Igor somehow got himself a job as a printer. It was always a great place to call in – a messy crumbling building, chaotically stacked with work in progress and with interesting people passing through.

TDATW were regularly getting gigs, and gradually in bigger venues – places like the Electric Ballroom in Camden. Without quite knowing how it happened we were invited to be part of a package of bands, including The Swell Maps and The Raincoats, that would play in Berlin later in the year. We were also invited to be one of a bunch of bands filmed playing live in a film studio in Battersea. I found the experience unnerving, observing myself on monitors as we played. We never got to see an edited version of the finished film.

A guy called Dick Witts from a band called The Passage, and who was also involved in the Manchester Musicians Collective, invited us to play in Manchester. In contrast to the LMC, the Manchester Musicians Collective was a collection of punk or punk-inspired bands. We hired a van and asked a friend to drive us up there. We roped Giblet in as a second guitar player, and took Grant with us to man the mixing desk, which was a labour of love on both their parts, since there was little money in it. The first band on were a great group of youngsters called Spurtz. They were charmingly inept four-piece with a female drummer called Corky. Having forgotten to turn up with his own instrument, Andy the guitarist borrowed mine, and I winced as he managed to drop it twice in the course of their short set. They were the opposite of The Passage who were headlining, who were very cerebral and professional. The most exciting thing about them was Dick's drumkit – he stood up to play behind an unusual selection of toms and small drums.

In the Engineer pub one night in the interval of a gig at the LMC Nag, Mark and I had run into Gareth Sager from The Pop Group. Gareth asked Mark what he was up to and then invited us to play supporting his band on their home turf in Bristol. Then he worried about his own idea – You're not a Grey band are you? I hate Grey music! We assumed he meant men in overcoats emulating Joy Division. No, we weren't, we reassured him. Gareth was drunk and we were unconvinced that the gig would happen, but a few weeks later, here we were on our way down to Bristol.

The Pop Group's second album *For How Much Longer Do We Tolerate Mass Murder?* had recently come out with its overtly political titles and ever more funky rhythms. Mark was very enthusiastic, even Nag was impressed. We were travelling to the gig in a van with some of the band and the Slits (who now shared the Pop Group's drummer), and their manager, Dick O'Dell. Giblet was playing with us and Grant was accompanying us to do the sound again.

We were playing Trinity Hall where we had played on the Weird Noise tour before Christmas. Only this time the place was packed. Looking out on the audience before we went on stage Nag and I were terrified. Grant offered to calm us down. He removed the magic mushroom shaped buckle from his belt and revealed that it was a hash pipe. Mark declined, but Nag and I boosted our confidence with Grant's drugs. The Pop Group were going to be playing with two drummers, and had both of their kits set up. We'd already agreed that Mark could use one of these and at the last minute had roped Dick in to play with us on the second kit. We managed to convert our nervous adrenalin into excited adrenalin and fed ourselves on the energy of the crowd, turning in a great performance that was met with enthusiastic applause from the audience.

On a high we joined the audience to dance crazily to the homecoming headliners; Giblet and me inviting ourselves onstage to join the band at the end of their set, before heading home in the van with the Slits again. Pausing at a motorway services in the early morning hours for refreshment we saw Viv making off with her food without paying for it: Do a runner! I stumbled into bed at home for a couple of hours before getting up for work at CCH.

And my work at CCH had provided me with a song of that title. I observed the residents complaining about the behaviour of the younger people who worked in the home, and the younger folk complaining about the attitudes of the old residents. I was convinced that both sets of people were essentially similar, just at different points in the same journey.

Street Level Again

We had booked more time in the cellar at the Street Level studios again with Grant at the controls. Although our album was still slowly working its way through the manufacturing process, we had plans to issue another release. Mark had ideas for two singles – the first would be put out under his name on Deptford Fun City, and the second released on NB records and credited to Mark Perry and Dennis Burns. The first was a cover of Ken Boothe's *The Whole World's Down On Me*, played by Mark and Dennis and Nag. The B side was a song of Mark's: *I Live He Dies* which included my attempts at becoming a drummer. The second single contained two songs *You Cry your Tears* and *Music Death*.

The tune for *Music Death* was inspired by Mark having heard the Janet and Johns perform their folk influenced music. It has a great repetitive drum beat played on one drum by Dave George from the Good Missionaries. *You Cry Your Tears* included the sounds of me and Anno, from Here And Now, doing what we were instructed to do by Mark, which was rolling around on the studio floor and weebling.

For the first single Mark had his girlfriend Lindsey take a picture of him for the cover, looking podgy and scruffy, but slightly cool with his Walkman headphones; and a picture of me, Anno, Nag, Mark, Dennis and Grant outside of Street Level on the back (roughly in order of height!). The NB records release would come in a plastic sleeve sandwiched between two pieces of 7X7 inch card, both printed on both sides. Mark provided really shitty looking pictures of himself and of Dennis, the one of himself possibly qualifying for worst ever record sleeve. On the inside Mark had typed some notes, mentioning that Dennis was "...enjoying life, and soon will start work on a duo album with Mark". When Dennis read it he said that he wasn't particularly enjoying life, so Mark just scribbled out those two words and we printed it without correction.

As NB Records we had started to pay Nag a wage. He'd been thrown off of the dole, so we agreed that we could afford to pay him a minimal wage for a while. When, after a few weeks, we realised how unsustainable this was, Nag simply signed on again, and didn't encounter any problems in doing so.

I wrote a song about managers and bosses – basically saying that bosses were the enemy. Igor did as he sometimes did - discussed and dissected the song, asking me what I really wanted to say. Managers, he pointed out to me, were not bad per se. It depended on how workplaces were organised – people could work as a co-op with a person elected as an overseer to make sure everything was done. He would quiz me, and then challenge my answers. Essentially he was tutoring me in clear thinking and improving my song-writing. My song about managers turned into a long political rant called Systems of Labour. I'm not sure that Igor approved of what I was saying, but at least he knew that it was well considered.

Improv

At one of the regular LMC monthly meetings we volunteered to help do some repairs. With (drummer) Roger Smith and (guitarist) Peter Cusack, I went up to inspect the roof space. There was a huge (non-functioning) ventilation tube running the length of the building, and the Co-op had complained about its conduction of sounds from our end of the building to theirs. We planned to saw through it where it passed through the partition, and then brick up the hole in the wall.

The following week Nag and I returned with Cy and Giblet to do the repairs. We accessed the loft space from a trap door above the lobby. It was a Saturday daytime and there were some people rehearsing in the main hall space, noodling away. The ceiling was high and to reach it we had positioned a huge but cronky old stepladder on top of a large table to get into the loft. Nag, who had somehow not realised that he needed to walk on the joists, stepped onto and straight through a sheet of plasterboard, luckily catching himself under each armpit. He hung there, perhaps 20 feet above the floor screaming. Cy and I were not strong enough to haul him up, so we climbed down the ladder and repositioned it and the table below Nags feet and helped him down. The improvisers in the next room must have taken Nag's cries for help as part of a performance, as they just kept on playing as we conducted our rescue.

Early on in our participation at the LMC we offended some of the members. We had produced a flyer for one of our gigs in the form of a strip cartoon. In it one person asks another if they want to come to a gig at the LMC, no, says the 2nd, it's full of old farts like Toop and Beresford. David and Steve found themselves being called old farts funny, but other members were upset and started to refer to Nag, Igor and myself as The Punks, seen to be causing trouble and bringing amplifiers into the building. In response to the upset we organised a series of discussion evenings, separate from the business meetings, where people could talk about music and ideology or anything they wanted to. At the first one we invited David Toop and Igor as speakers.

Having reassured some of our detractors by doing this we then upset people again. We volunteered to re-paint the performance space. Rather than just paint it, we thought we'd turn it into a performance and produced flyers for a "paint/music dichotomy" event. We turned up on the evening with Cy, Giblet and Chris, with a few others, some instruments and loads of paint and rollers. We hooted and tooted and began to put paint on the walls. We'd pour a tin of paint into a tray, and then when it was running low add another tin, of another hue to the tray, so that gradually the whole room was transformed into an abstract painting. A small number of people arrived as audience members. We didn't bother to collect any entrance fee. They wandered around for a bit and then left. Painting the large space took longer than anticipated, and some of our crew left for home. We'd been drinking tins of beer and Nag was now drunk. He started to paint football scores on the walls, until we confiscated his brush and told him to go to sleep. Whilst he dozed Cy and Giblet and I worked through the night.

A couple of days later Igor suggested that I listen to the answering machine. One of the LMC members had left a furious message – what had we bastards done to his space? He threatened to kill us. We went back to inspect our decoration, and had to admit that it was a little messy. We carefully painted the skirting boards white, to make it look properly finished off. I was scared, wary of the angry member turning up to assault us, but he failed to appear at our house. Other members also disliked our multi-coloured walls and someone repainted the whole space white.

We did, however also make friends. Some of the older LMC members realised that the place couldn't remain static and were also open to a range of musics. Early on we had connected with Steve and David and also with their partners in Whirled Music – Max Eastley and Paul Burwell. Whirled Music were a group who did what the name suggests. Wearing protective wickerwork helmets they'd whiz noise making devices round their heads. Their performances were slightly unpredictable, dangerous events sometimes dull, sometimes alarming and funny. Out of performance, Max, Steve and David were genteel polite men in their early thirties. Paul was always slightly dangerous and unpredictable. In one performance with him he began to shout at me when I hit one of his toy drums too hard and split a skin. Turning the argument into part of the performance, Giblet began to shout back. Paul flipped Giblet across the stage with a judo throw, leaving him and the rest of us a little alarmed and wary. Although he was small he could be scary. Thankfully he had a great sense of humour and was a supportive friend.

We were also friendly with drummer Terry Day, Sax player Lol Coxhill and with Peter Cusack. Giblet separately made contact with these folk and invited them to take part in the 49 Americans. The 49 Americans swelled into a large pool of players, the oldest of whom were twice the age of the youngest. I found this inspiring – after writing *Dads*, and believing that over a certain age people became creatively dead, here was evidence to the contrary, and hope for myself as I got older. The LMC members who became part of the 49 Americans were also amazing with their generosity of spirit. Professional musicians in their mid-thirties, treating upstarts like Nag and I, and schoolkids like Else as equals.

```
┌─────────────────────────┬──────────────────────────┐
│ THE 49                  │                          │
│ AMERICANS               │                          │
│ A way of sending        │                          │
│ sounds over a long      ├──────────────────────────┤
│ distance by means       │ THE MAJORCA              │
│ of electrical waves     │ ORCHESTRA                │
│ without connecting      │                          │
│ wires.                  │ Friendly toward          │
├──────────────┬──────────┤ company; enjoy-          │
│ £1.00        │          │ ing entertaining         │
│ £1.25        │          │ people.                  │
│ (NON-MEMBERS)│          │                          │
│              │          ├──────────────────────────┤
│ A device     │          │ AT THE LONDON MUSICIAN'S │
│ to take the  │          │ COLLECTIVE (42 GLOUCESTER AVE. │
│ water out    │          │             N.W.1 CAMDEN TOWN) │
│ of wet       │          │ An enclosure in which    │
│ clothes.     │          │ energy in a non-thermal  │
├──────────────┴──────────┤ form is converted to     │
│                         │ heat.                    │
├─────────────────────────┼─────────────┬────────────┤
│ TUESDAY,                │             │ 8:00pm     │
│ JULY 1st                │             │            │
│ A mark, stain,          │             │ Romp and   │
│ blot, or speck.         │             │ play happily. │
└─────────────────────────┴─────────────┴────────────┘
```

We organised joint gigs at the LMC for Alterations (Steve, David, Terry and Peter) and TDATW. Peter always intrigued Nag and I. Chairing LMC meetings he would stutter and oscillate with a nervous tremor so much that we would also feel nervous. But in performance he had no shake and would play delicate and precise parts on his acoustic guitar. Some of the plinky-plonk (as Steve called it) at the LMC would drive us nuts – this "free" music seemed to have its own instrument specific clichés. If a performance bored us, we found that we could end it by applauding wildly at one of the quiet moments. Or I might try to baffle performers into silence by emulating Cy and setting my hair alight. Alterations kept our attention with their sense of humour and their lack of pretension.

Twang

A friend of Vicky's called Debbie had arrived in London earlier in the year. She had moved into the squatted flat with Vicky, and they had both moved into a flat with Keith and his brother Kevin when a mass eviction of the squatters from their previous residence had happened. But the two women couldn't cope with a double dose of the Allen brothers' laddish energy and moved out. They asked Igor and Nag and I if they could temporarily move into our rehearsal room whilst they found themselves proper accommodation. We agreed and they moved a double mattress and a few belongings in for a while.

Vicky living in the same building didn't lead to any more intensity in our relationship, we carried on the same, spending time with each other when we both wanted to.

Grant was the regular sound guy for The Fall. He got Mark and Nag and I in on the guest list for a gig at the Electric Ballroom, and then regretted it when Nag and I tried to commandeer the mixing desk whilst the Fall were playing.

The album was ready! The sleeves looked great and were printed on high quality card. We'd listed the tracks as being on either the green side or the red side, and had had the album pressed with a plain label on each side in those colours. This meant that it was the first record that we didn't have to stick on little labels by hand with the track listing. Including those that Rough Trade took as part of the M & D deal, we sold 700 in the first week, which meant that we were negotiating the pressing of a second thousand almost immediately.

We took a copy of the album to John Peel, and accompanied him to the pub with another Radio One DJ called Kid Jensen, along with Bruce Gilbert and Graham Lewis of Wire, who were also producing records as a duo under the name of Dome. The slightly sleazy-seeming Kid Jensen was tailed by some fawning female fans, and they joined our group. He and Peel seemed keen to engage with them, posing for photos. Gilbert and Lewis seemed to be able to deal with this showbiz slime but we passed on our copy of the album and left.

Peel played our version of the TV Personalities *Part Time Punks* that evening. The original was a witty critique of trend following pseudo punks, and we'd updated the references to bands to make the content current, and we'd sung it (badly on my part) over a sparse drum beat.

Fritz got in touch and said that Skidoo wanted their echo machine back, and we duly returned it. The next time we heard them they were amazing – their music had developed into a kind of toxic-edged funk. We were very impressed by how much they had changed and improved. Rehearsing at the same venue, Igor's band were getting good, and they expanded their line-up with a cellist called Kate, a friend of the Tufnell Park Mob.

Out in the world at large the SAS stormed the Iranian Embassy in London and ended the siege that had lasted several days since a number of armed men had taken over the building, and had killed one of their hostages.

Vicky and Debbie found themselves some furnished rented accommodation and had moved out. Because she didn't need it, Vicky gave her horsehair mattress to me, and so my bed got more comfortable. Vicky was excited because some friends of hers, a band called the Birthday Party had arrived in London from Melbourne. She was keen to introduce us, but we knew that some of them were using heroin, and we didn't want to be around them.

Nag and I had one of our regular Friday meetings with Mark, starting at Faulty and going on to Mike's café. We had a number of gigs coming up, and Mark said that he wanted to step back a bit. He felt uncomfortable with the typical band scenario of putting out records and doing lots of gigs. He said that he would do the next booking, at the Centro Iberico, with us but that he would drop out of the four gigs subsequent to that. He reassured us that he wasn't leaving, just that he wanted a month off.

On that Friday we had found a skip near to the Faulty offices, that was full of small coloured pieces of wood. About an inch tall, they were shaped like chess pawns, but were in five different colours. We guessed that they were markers for some sort of board game, and that perhaps the makers had gone bust. I filled a carrier bag with them, and took them into my handyman's room at CCH the following Monday. Then, over the coming days and weeks I started to hide them all around the building in obscure locations, with no intention other than mystifying whoever would later find them.

The Centro Iberico gig was an evening split into two parts: first there was a showing of the Bunuel film *Simon of the Desert*, and then the bands playing. Dennis was in the band for this gig, and after setting up our gear the four of us went to a local pub. We joined the audience for the film. I'd heard a lot about the surrealist film maker, but not seen any of his films. I was surprised to find myself bored, as were Mark and Dennis. The three of us left and returned to the pub, leaving Nag to watch the film. Nag had had too much to drink already, and sat numbly watching the screen. We came back to the venue when the film had finished. The organisers had sold separate tickets for the film and the music and were evicting the whole audience, before re-admitting those who wanted to see us play. Nag emerged looking pained and dishevelled. When we asked him what was up he said that the man sitting next to him had thumped him. Why? - because I vomited on him!

Purged of his alcohol, Nag was in good form for the performance and we were all happy playing together as a quartet.

An idea of Garry's for Chain of Dots was that we'd play a tape of the 60's hit *Anyone Who Had a Heart* before the band played, to set the right atmosphere for us to perform. We had modified his idea, making sure we had a tape to give to DJ's to play before we came on. We might get them to play something very heavy by This Heat, or something silly like a tune by Lonnie Donegan. Derisive of the pantomime of bands playing encores, we would often leave the stage with a tape running that would undermine any potential for this happening: Did you enjoy yourselves?...Did you have a good time? - looped over and over again.

The next gig a week later was at The Tabernacle in Notting Hill. We had organised the gig collectively with the other bands playing the bill – the Desperate Bicycles, Nick Turner's Inner City Unit and the Murphy's. We were to be a quartet again, but this time the line-up was to be with Else on drums and Giblet playing bass.

All of the bands had pooled equipment and responsibilities. Early on in the evening I was on the door checking tickets and taking people's money. A big mean looking biker strode up and said – I get in free. I explained that it was a low price for admission, that it was a co-operative venture, and that no-one got in free. He said that we'd see about that. I was expecting him to push past or to hit me, but he walked away. For a moment I felt relief, but he turned to face me and said – I'll be back, and I'm going to sort you. I spent the rest of my shift on the door nervously awaiting his return, but saw no sign of him.

Inside the venue there was a really good party atmosphere. When we took the stage we found that we'd become a six piece. Welcome, though uninvited, we had been joined again by Roddy Disorder and the anonymous trombone player. And we were great! People were dancing. Then I noticed the mean biker at the front of the crowd, shaking his fist at me. I just smiled, and felt invulnerable, elevated a couple of feet above him on the stage, and filled with the energy of performing. By the end of our set he was dancing along with the rest of the crowd.

When I later related the story of the mean biker to our friend Scottish Tim, who had been at the gig, he said, well it was probably the acid. Busy with our duties and with performing we had been oblivious of the sale of some cheap but good quality LSD at the venue. Tim reckoned that half of the audience was tripping.

The gig after that was also in London, at the 101 club in Clapham – which was packed full. We played as a three piece band with Igor as a surprisingly good drummer. Towards the end of the performance we became a four piece when I found myself unable to sing and play my guitar simultaneously. I passed my guitar to Nic from Igor's band, who was in the audience, and carried on singing. I reclaimed the guitar for the end of our set where without Mark we performed one of his songs. When we finished playing there was a moment of silence, then half the audience applauded loudly, and the other half booed loudly. Playing back the tape afterwards we could hear Grant, who had been mixing, joining in with the disapproving half of the audience – Rubbish! Get off! Charles Bullen from This Heat was in the audience. Speaking with him afterwards he said it was one of the most intense performances that he had witnessed, and certainly the most polarised reaction from an audience. I liked the word intense – and coming from a member of This Heat it felt like a huge compliment.

Romance

I'd met a girl called Gunilla at the Fall gig where we had messed with the sound, and had subsequently met up with her and had a brief spell of going out together. But neither of us really clicked with each other, and we mutually drifted apart. I started going out with Kate the cellist, and we'd meet up before or after Take It performances. She was still at school, and her parents were less easy than Nicola's had been about her staying the night with me. And to make it harder for Kate, she had to cope with the message on my ceiling. After splitting with Nicola I had painted my bedroom in camouflage–like abstract patches of greens and brown. On the ceiling I had painted a circle, and within it the words – Are you sleeping in the right bed?

Igor, working part time at Better Badges somehow seemed to be going out with or trying to chat up three women at the same time. Confusingly all of them were called Sarah. One of the Sarahs was performing in a duo with Jim from the School House. Also confusingly Jim was now known as Amos. Amos had been a member of The Homosexuals, and was a very talented musician working under a variety of different names, such as L Voag, making obscure experimental pop music. Working as a duo, Amos and Sarah put out a series of brilliant quirky cassette albums.

Nag, for reason's unknown to me, was no longer going out with Else. All of his relationships had indistinct edges, a new romance tending to begin before the old one had ended. Now he was going out with Etta.

And Giblet was courting Else.

More Gigs

We were rehearsing with the 49 Americans at Steve Beresford's house. Steve ended up supplying a lot of the instruments that the band played. With Alterations he would often play toy instruments, and those are what some of us in the band ended up playing. There were a couple of small battery-operated keyboards that I played and also some toy pianos. We played at the LMC and also at a couple of community fayres, including one in Primrose Hill. The public liked our wonky, slightly off-key pop music, and from little kids to old ladies, they enthused.

Charles and Hywell had squatted a big building in the rather upmarket Delancy Street in Camden. They said that we could use their basement as a rehearsal space, complete with drum kit and amplifiers. With Mark back on board we went to investigate. From the street outside I looked through the iron railings and down into the room we were to be using. I pointed out to the other two that there were two skinheads down there playing music. I was rather scared, but Mark encouraged us down. We knocked on the door and were met by two very gentle skinheads. They knew that we were due to arrive and passed the space over to us. They explained that they knew Charles and Hywell from Wales, and were two members of a band called Young Marble Giants.

We had a gig just outside of London at Ravensbourne College of Art, with Alterations and Lol Coxhill. The venue was a big impersonal space, and the stage was made of separate blocks, so that when we performed each of the three of us was on their own little island of a stage, with the PA speakers way off to the side. We were on first, and inhibited by the space, failed to connect completely with each other and with the audience. Lol and the guys from Alterations felt the same about the venue as we did. At the end I and Lol joined in with Alterations, and we made a big cathartic noise, but none of us really enjoyed the experience. We got paid well, though!

Visiting Rough Trade on a Friday we found a poster on the door advertising a gig where the billing was Dome, DAF and us. No-one had asked us! We liked the idea of playing with Gilbert & Lewis, and DAF, an electronic German duo (to whom we had been introduced by Vicky) were great, but we hadn't been asked, and the admission charge was too much. We got a piece of paper and stuck a note onto the poster saying that TDATW thought that £2.50 was a bloody ridiculous admission charge and that we would not be playing.

The negotiations around the gig in Berlin had been dragging on. We had a meeting with a couple of the Swell maps and with Shirley, the Raincoats' manager. She phoned and spoke to the promoters in Germany. There was some kind of confusion and argument about the fees and suddenly the gig was off.

A year or so after our first LMC gig we played at the same venue to a packed audience at what turned into a great celebratory gig. We planned that TDATW would headline, and for the support acts each of us would form a new band for a one-off performance. I got together with Simon Pearce and Roddy Disorder to do a piece based on the short Beckett play *That Time*. Nag played with David Toop and Giblet; and Mark played with Dennis and also his friends Sam and Dave from the Transmitters. Each of our three temporary bands played very different music, all equally well received: Nag and co played wonky cover versions of pop songs including *Why Don't We Do It In The Road* and *Oh Bondage Up Yours*. Mark's group played experimental rock, and my trio's performance was a semi-improvised musical play, with all three of us speaking and singing as different aspects of the same character.

Dennis played with us as part of TDATW, and we played long exploratory versions of some of our regular songs, including a very protracted version of Dads. I had written a song called *Lust*, critical of the way in which my interactions with women were always being subverted with sexual thoughts. Live we performed it with a noodly introduction with Mark and I whispering and flirting with each other, and him playing little bits of saxophone before seating himself at the drumkit for the thrashy heart of the song: *Lust gets in the way sometimes, lust gets in the fucking way!* With the line-up that we had planned for the evening there were lots of spare instruments around, and at some point David Toop walked up and joined in on guitar, and then gradually more and more of the audience joined in. We played a long improvised song with Nag singing – *everyone joined the LMC that year, oh what a year that was,* – as the band gradually swelled in number. And then the band gradually got smaller as people left to catch last buses and tube trains. But we were ecstatic and just carried on for as long as the music needed to be played.

After meeting up at Faulty one week, Nag and Mark went on elsewhere and I popped into Rough Trade. It seemed to be a day when all the people in the shop were people involved in making music. One after another, or merging into each other I had conversations with a couple of members of the Desperate Bicycles and of a band called The Different I's; Daniel Miller, Nick Turner and Dick O'Dell. Then a band called Contact came into the shop. They had come all the way from Manchester to play a gig that had been cancelled. Did any of us know of a gig that night that they might tag onto. Despite the range of people in the shop, nobody knew of any events occurring that evening. I offered that if there was nothing else happening then perhaps they could do something low key at a place I knew called the School House. I scrounged access to a phone and called Rob, yes they would accommodate the band. They had a van, so I jumped in and directed them down to Hammersmith.

I'd been popping in on the School House people on evenings when they put on gigs or plays that they had written, and had joined in a couple of times with spontaneously formed bands. Tonight a number of people who were around were willing to add some other acts to the bill and to contact friends so that there was an audience. Contact were pleased that at least they had somewhere to be, and I got to perform in a quartet singing and playing guitar with Roddy, Rob and someone whose name failed to register who played a piano.

Beat the Tory Blues

In the middle of June a huge one day festival called Beat the Blues took place, organised by The Morning Star and conveniently situated for us within walking distance from home at Ally Pally. A day of cultural resistance to uplift people in the face of increasing inequality under the Tory government, it featured political speakers as well as musical acts. It was a sunny day and a great festival. Snotcher came up to London to attend, and we wandered around meeting loads of friends. Mostly it was people from London that I met, but also Garry Bailey was there, having travelled down with Mark Automaton. The air was full of the smell of barbecued lamb, and I introduced Snotcher to his first Pizza.

Acts included The Raincoats and John Cooper Clarke but for me the musical highlights were seeing the Slits and the Pop Group on one after the other, with Bruce Smith bouncing away behind the drum kit for both bands.

One day I went into work. I'd been feeling stretched trying to do the job and keep up my musical life. On this particular day I saw one of the staff reading a copy of the Sun newspaper. I had an argument with him about reading such crap, and in a bad mood without thinking walked into the Matron's office and gave a week's notice to quit.

There was a weekend festival at the LMC featuring guitar players. There had been much discussion and dispute at the monthly meetings about the rights and wrongs of having a festival that promoted one instrument. Nag and I avoided getting involved – we felt that if someone wanted to organise a particular event and were willing to invest the energy, then let them get on with it. But there was only so much Art's Council money per year, was the response. Hmmm, that old rubbish again. We felt it was good to have funding for the building but that gigs should pay for themselves.

Toop and Beresford were playing a set at the guitar festival. They invited me to be a guest performer at the end of their bit. When it came to it they seemed to be taking the piss out of the event and hardly seemed to play guitars at all. They did at the end when I was invited "on stage" (there was no stage) to join them. I was embarrassed and awkward and no asset to their sound.

At the end of June the Mark/Dennis singles were ready, and the pair of them came round to Ferrestone road to sleeve them up. The four of us spent an intense five hours and managed to get them all done.

We put out a live TDATW album on cassette, called Music and Movement, containing a mixture of old and new songs, and we had plans for another project. We spent some time with Igor recording some songs at home. The idea was that we would release a compilation EP of songs supposedly by four French bands. We wrote funny words about radical philosophers and thinkers like Foucault and Derrida (whom Igor was reading, but whom Nag and I failed to understand), and translated them as best we could into French, and then spoke or sang them along with our tunes.

A few people had mentioned to us about publishing our songs, but we hadn't really done anything about it. We wrote "published by NB Records" on releases, but didn't understand the process. We failed to receive any money for our songs being played on Radio One and Capital Radio. In turn no-one asked us about royalties for the TV Personalities song that we had covered, but we got some advice about how much would normally have been paid. We wrote out a cheque and I went down to a tower block near the King's Road to deliver it personally to Dan the leader of the band. He had heard Peel play it and was delighted that we had done a cover version. He was also delighted that we'd bothered to pay him.

Jazz Punk Bonanza

Giblet and Nag came up with their own idea of a festival at the LMC, and we spent July organising it. We dubbed it The Jazz Punk Bonanza, and set it to run over three nights. None of the groups playing were jazz bands, none were punk. The conjunction of the two words perhaps described the music of one of the bands on the first night's bill – Dislocation Dance from Manchester, but mostly we liked it because the two words together felt slightly wrong. Igor got the job of printing some large posters for the event at Better Badges and threatened that if we upset him he would change the wording to read Jazz-Funk!

Alterations headed up the bill on the Friday night. The place was packed – we'd generated a much bigger audience than they would normally have – and a different one. They seemed a little wary of getting a bad reaction from an audience more attuned to some variant of rock music, and gave a little self-conscious introduction and an explanation that they didn't play tunes. Actually, the way in which they responded to the audience was great, David playing bass, and the band unusually for them, playing grooves. Steve had played on tour as a guest member of the Slits, and Viv was in the audience, one of a number of people quickly dancing.

Dislocation Dance had given a polished performance, and Spurtz who had travelled down with them were much more together than when we had played with them in Manchester – but they still had a this-could-all-fall-apart-at-any-moment charm.

We'd invited The Instant Automatons down to play on the Sunday, and the PA was a mix of Cy and Protag's gear. We were learning that Protag was an easy to get along with Mr Fix It. If he was operating the mixing desk, his response to any criticism of what he was doing was to politely ask how he might make things better. Cy was more like a bomb ready to go off – if a musician was stroppy with him, or if he perceived them to be, he would be ratty back. Nag and Giblet and I were diligently acting as mediators and middlemen between him and the bands, but he had already pissed off Alterations on the first night.

Bendle

One or two of us were camping out at the LMC all weekend, keeping an eye on the equipment. On the Friday I had gone home to sleep. Travelling back early on Saturday afternoon I saw huge black storm clouds billowing up in the sky against a backdrop that turned from blue to a weird shade of yellow. I'd never seen a sky like it. Arriving at the LMC I found that Protag had been so un-nerved by what he took to be indication of the beginning of a nuclear war that he had phoned his Mum to say that he loved her. The yellow in the sky turned to purple and our feared nuclear holocaust transpired to just be a thunderstorm. Mark from the Automatons told me that the pendant on a chain round his neck contained a cyanide pill. If it came to a Third World War, he would take the pill.

Saturday night and we had a queue up the stairs again. The headline band were the Lemon Kittens, a band that Mark had briefly drummed with before joining TDATW. The core of the band were a man called Karl and a woman called Danielle. They had both been attending LMC meetings and had become our friends over the summer. Their performances were almost violently intense, but their weird songs also had a surreal humour to them.

We had placed TDATW second on the bill for that evening. It felt great to be playing to a sell-out crowd in a venue where initially we had played to a handful of people.

Dennis, Bendle, Nag, Mark Picture Mark Lancaster

The Automatons played on the Sunday, along with Take It, who had developed into a band with great dance inducing songs. Igor also started the evening off playing under the guise of Pretentious Art Forms, doing a send up of the improv that normally happened at the venue, which was only understood by a minority of the audience. The headline act that night was billed as Low Flying Aircraft. This was a duo of Paul Burwell and Anne Bean, who possibly thought of the name of their band as being PULp Music.

Paul and Anne had recorded a single in 1979 with Paul drumming and Anne singing over and over that *there's a low flying aircraft, a low flying aircraft* – with one side simply being a continuation of the other. They had gotten a thousand singles pressed up, in plain white sleeves, with no label. Some of them they left like this, some of them they carefully decorated, others they just scrawled on. Lots of the copies had an extra hole burned through, just off centre, so that it could be played eccentrically. I'm not sure that any of them included the name of the band nor of the title of the music. It felt like a great mix of punk and avant garde. They had taken a few hundred copies of the single and just dumped them at Rough Trade, with no explanation, and from this had generated sales and radio play without people knowing who they were. Their ending the festival meant that a big audience got to see Paul and Anne doing one of their crazed anything goes performances, and a glimpse of normal activity at the LMC.

The whole weekend had been a great success, musically, spiritually and financially, and the small gang of us that were sleeping over on the Sunday night sat around drinking beer and celebrating the weekend, before cleaning everything up on the Monday morning.

The Automatons had decided to put out a double compilation single, and we returned to Street Level to record a version of CCH, with Dennis playing saxophone.

On Tour in Europe

Disappointed that the Berlin gig had fallen through Nag and I had planned a three week holiday in Europe. I felt that Nag and I had been getting on top of each other – working together and socialising together. We'd alternate from being totally in synch to being ratty with each other. We'd not discussed this, but it seemed to me that going away together might be a good thing – no work, just play – or conversely that it might mark a crisis and a change in our relationship.

We had had (mail) orders for records from all around Europe, and we compiled a list of names and addresses of people who had purchased our music. We planned to get the train/boat to Amsterdam, and from there hitch our way round, calling in on names on our list. Since we didn't have a planned route, and didn't know how successful our hitching would be, we didn't think there was any point in alerting anyone that we might turn up on them.

Near the beginning of August we packed my little Force Ten tent and set off, enduring the squalid boat crossing from Harwich to Hook van Holland. I found that the only way that I could avoid feeling sea sick was to stay on deck, so we spent the night crossing either standing at the rails watching the big jellyfish wash past the boat, or trying to sleep in our sleeping bags on benches on deck. I thought back to the night before. I had been invited out by an American woman called Page who worked in Compendium Books. She had taken me to a poetry reading in a small room above a bar. I'd never been to such a thing before and was expecting pious readings of verse. What I actually got to hear sounded more like flow of consciousness washes of words, in which I got lost, and by which I was inspired. The evening was running late, and to get home I had to leave before the end. I'd whispered this to Page, who wanted to stay listening. A poet called Chris Cheek was reading. I stood up and tried to discreetly make my way out of the small audience. Chris, who until that point had been unknown to me, stopped reading and said – Goodnight Bendle. I had muttered a goodnight in reply to him and the turned faces of the other punters, wondering how on earth he knew who I was.

We arrived bleary eyed in Amsterdam and were welcomed by a flock of starlings perched on trees near the station. We decided that travel by tram was free since there seemed to be no one to check that we had purchased tickets and we wandered the city. We visited a bar and were disappointed by the large price tag and the fact that the barman swiped all of the foam off of the top of our beers with a wooden spatula. We felt that we had been swindled out of whatever volume of beer was contained in the head.

We made our way to our first contact. Someone called Hans Hauser had purchased a single from us. We found the flat and knocked at the door. A late-middle aged man answered and we said (in English) that we were looking for Hans – did he live here? Yes, said the man and invited us in. We sat, as invited, on a settee and the man sat on a chair facing us. We sat waiting in awkward silence for Hans to appear, until the man said – I am Hans! We had been expecting a teenager or someone at least half his age. He gave us tea which we sweetened with large confectionery crystals of sugar, which I had never seen before. We explained that we were The Door and The Window – he had bought our single – yes? He had, though we didn't know why – all of his other records seemed to be Tamla Motown. In broken English he told us about himself. He had worked all of his life in a biscuit and sweet factory and had recently either retired or been made redundant – we couldn't quite work out which. His payoff had included a heap of biscuits on which he seemed to be living. He was proud of the fact that he had come by most of his furnishings from other people's junk. He explained that this was a wealthy neighbourhood, and that people threw out perfectly good things. Most of what he owned had been taken from next to people's dustbins. He was looking after the flat next door whilst his next door neighbour was away, and if we were careful of the property we could sleep there for a couple of nights.

We took up Hans' offer, wandering the streets of Amsterdam in the daytime, and returning in the evening to Hans and his neighbour's flat. A young man wandered up to us somewhere in the middle of city and asked us, in English, did we want to buy some hash? No, sorry we didn't. Insulted by this, he produced a small knife and pointed it at my belly – we did want to buy some hash – yes? Well, perhaps we would have a little. He produced a lump from his pocket, cut us a small piece and wrapped it in a paper handkerchief. He took our proffered guilders, passed us the hanky and then suddenly said that he had spotted the police, and he ran away. We looked around for possible policemen, but there were none. When we unwrapped the tissue it was empty.

We had little idea of what to look for in Amsterdam, but were keen to avoid the usual tourist attractions. We found our way to a park on the edge of town where we watched two enormous sea lions mating, and then discovered a little walled garden. As we looked around the garden I was intrigued to see that most of the plants growing there were poisonous. In my teens, living in Swindon, I had been keen to investigate intoxication with cannabis. I had failed to find any source for the drug until just before I left for Matlock and had started to look for indigenous narcotic plants. Top of my list had been Thornapple. I had never found any, but, now, here it was, in a border next to Henbane and Deadly Nightshade. I picked some leaves, but knew that soon we would be travelling South, and that I didn't want to risk being stopped at the border with them. We also spotted something else that I recognised, but had never seen before – a giant puffball (mushroom). We picked it and took it back to cook for supper with Hans.

Hans told us where to start hitching towards Germany. We had two good lifts taking us to a town called Venlo, on the border. The man who dropped us there said sorry, but he could not go any closer to Germany – he was still too haunted by what the Germans had done in the war. We walked through the border without any hassle and started to hitch on a slip road of a motorway. We had only a very tiny pocket atlas of Europe and were not really sure of the best routes to where we were heading. Dortmund was the next address on our list.

A police car stopped next to us and one of the officers grilled us. We said that we couldn't speak German. Passports! Demanded the policeman. When we proffered our passports the man grabbed them and the police car sped away with our documents. Shocked, we wondered what to do? Call the police? We stood fretting for five minutes, at which point the police drove up from behind us, passed us back our passports and drove off again, laughing.

Our progress was much slower than it had been in Holland. We got into Duisburg in the evening and ate a cold pizza which we found in a bin. We caught a tram to the edge of town and slept in my tent in a field.

The next day we made our way by tram and hitching to Dortmund. Again it seemed that we didn't need to pay on the trams. Knocking at the door at the address in Dortmund we were answered by a man who could speak English. We asked after our fan – the man's son. We explained who we were and the man forcefully told us to get lost. One success, one failure!

We had another contact in Ratingen, near Düsseldorf. Looking at our map, it seemed to be most of the way back towards Venlo. We were disheartened, but wanted to check this person out – she was called Rosi and we were drawn to her by the lipstick kiss that she'd put on the letters when ordering records. We got onto a train from Dortmund to Düsseldorf, without tickets. We were found by a ticket inspector part way along our route. We feigned not understanding that he wanted our tickets, but were evicted from the train at the next station.

Hitching into Düsseldorf we made our way by bus to Ratingen. Rosi was in! She could speak no English, we could speak no German. She seemed to understand who we were and invited us in. She found a young boy from next door who could speak English and who explained to us that Rosi had phoned her boyfriend and he was on his way. That the boyfriend could speak English. And did we like Pizza? Rosi gave us tea and a while later Nag and I were bemused by the delivery to the property of a Pizza. We were disappointed by mention of a boyfriend, but were being well looked after.

The boyfriend was called Ziggy. He turned up dressed in a suit and explained that he worked in a bank. He loved our music and was very excited that we had turned up. He said that he had bought our records but thought that he would make a better connection with us if Rosi signed the letters. He would take the afternoon off of work and take us to meet some more fans of TDATW.

He drove us to the small town of Krefeld and to a quiet record shop called Between Sale and Zdrk[ii] . As we entered the shop we realised that they were playing our music – was that the first single? No, it was from Permanent Transience. We didn't know that copies of the tape had travelled outside of the UK. The shop was run by some boys about our age called Klaus and Wolfgang, who were very excited by our arrival.

The shop had some shelves of records round the edge – they sold only industrial music and reggae – and two small settees in the middle both facing a coffee table. Customers were welcome to browse and to sit at the table eating chocolate and drinking free coffee whilst they listened to records over the shop's high quality music system. We quickly decided that it was the world's best record shop, and better still we were guests of honour. Klaus and Wolfgang went out to buy food for us – they decided that we should be fed fresh fruit and beer. Another friend of theirs called Jurgen turned up and we spent the afternoon drinking and eating, and chatting. They all spoke English well. At the end of the afternoon Ziggy went home leaving us with our new friends. Jurgen drove us back to his house where he said we could stay.

That evening Wolfgang, who had come back with us asked – would you like a little bit of shit? Shit? Shit was their word for hash. The smoke from that evening seemed to fog our subsequent days in and around Krefeld and Düsseldorf, where our drugged perception gave Nag and I the impression that everyone in Düsseldorf was stoned. We spent time with our hosts and also time wandering around on our own. We visited the Düsseldorf aquarium and marvelled at the colourful fish with our cannabis enhanced vision. In the evenings Wolfgang or Ziggy would drive us around the Ruhr, the car leaving a trail of cannabis smoke. We'd join our friends in their favourite spots listening to the rhythmic percussive "music" emanating from industrial plants. Would we like to go for a trip? Wolfgang had asked us. We had thought that perhaps he meant a trip facilitated by psychedelics, but when the day came he drove us all round the region sightseeing. Then that evening he and his friends offered us another trip, this time with LSD.

At one of Wolfgang's friend's houses we swallowed our tiny black tablets and spent the first part of the evening playing music. They had synths and guitars and lots of effects pedals. There were about ten of us altogether, four or five of them women. For some reason only the men took the LSD, but the women were carried along in the same psychic state. After a while the normal world faded away to be replaced by another made of spinning colours and lights. After an age or two Nag and I would reconnect with each other, and the others in the room, then off we'd go to some other universe. At one point we were all in one room. Someone pointed to a candle on the far side of the room and as we all looked it lit itself.

When the effects were wearing off Ziggy drove us back to his and Rosi's place and we tried to sleep the rest of the night. When I got up in the morning and went to the toilet I found that all of the small tiles in the bathroom were moving around and that my perception was still influenced by the acid. Nag and I tried to regain some sense of normality as Ziggy drove us to a good spot to hitch south and continue our journey.

We were lucky. We got a lift from a young man who could speak English, and who drove us a long way, past Koln and Bonn, on and on towards Karlsruhe. The car was an old battered 2CV. It was a hot day, but the heater in the car was jammed on full. We travelled with the windows wide open, but still felt like we were cooking. We stopped to pick up some snacks and then our host continued south. He offered us beer from bottles lying near our feet, but they were hot from the heater. The radio in the car was also broken and would tune itself to whichever station was strongest. Every now and again we would get a German station, but often we also got local forces radio transmitted to NATO army units. American and English voices accompanied our journey. It gave me the impression of Germany being full of NATO soldiers, and made me very aware of Germany as the buffer between the East and West.

We were shattered. Our host was travelling on, but we asked to get out and to find a place to sleep. We walked across a field to try to get away from the noise of the autobahn, erected my little tent in a stupidly visible place and crawled into our sleeping bags. The air was thick with little midges, and, tormented by their bites, Nag wrapped his head in a towel and went to sleep.

The next day we felt ourselves to be more firmly back in everyday reality. We hitched more slowly but managed to get to Konstanz and crossed over the border into Switzerland. We entered a camp site late in the evening and settled into our tent as a huge thunderstorm played out over the Alps. We rose early and left without paying and wandered Westwards. A lift left us near the western end of Lake Konstanz and I decided to take a swim. I swam out some way, then realised with horror that I was being pulled downstream by the current into the Rhine. I managed to swim to the shore and made my way back to Nag, a little shaken. We went to a shop which accepted our German currency in lieu of Swiss and bought a few items to eat. Shocked by how much things cost, we decided that we needed to get out of Switzerland as quickly as possible.

Hitching through the day we arrived in Basle that evening, very hungry. We wandered around looking for something like a chip shop, but couldn't find one. We looked for a cheap cafe or restaurant, but reading menus in windows found that we couldn't afford them. We ended up finding a rough pub near the Rhine that seemed to be inhabited by blokes that crewed vessels up and down the river. We ordered a cheap pasta dish each and settled down to eat. Waiting for our meal we were accosted by the inhabitants of the bar. They offered us hard boiled eggs that seemed to be available as appetisers from the bar, and then tried to make us eat cigarettes sprinkled with salt. Nag and I were scared of these mean muscled men and were trying to figure out how to escape, when we were rescued by the woman serving our meals. Saying something that we took to mean leave these boys alone, she brushed the men out of the way and gave us our food. We ate quickly and escaped. We walked and just kept walking until we had crossed the border into France, and slept once again in a field near the road.

We decided to head for Marseilles where we had the address of a radio DJ who liked our music. We hitched a lift to Mulhouse, but realised that we had travelled north. We decided to head initially towards Lyon, but had difficulty getting lifts. Both of us could speak a little French, so at last we had more chance of communicating with the people around us.

Stuck at a little junction a farmer offered a lift on his trailer to a much better to place to get a lift. We took up his offer, dumping our rucksacks on the floor of the trailer and standing up holding onto the rail at the front. He drove us down smaller and smaller roads. We kept expecting to cross a junction from where we could pick up some long-distance traffic, but eventually the farmer dropped us at a tiny crossroads in the middle of nowhere. He pointed out a small bar where he said we could eat cheaply. In the absence of being able to travel easily any further we took his advice and ate pasta with "wild beast of the forest" - was this deer? Wild pig? The rich sauce made the meat impossible to identify.

We walked for some miles, despondent about getting back to a proper road, but in good humour with each other. We made it back to a main road, but for the next two days waited ages between lifts, and when we got one they didn't take us very far. We got dropped in Besançon, which seemed to be a town from the middle ages peppered with a few tower blocks dropped into the 20th century. Somewhere a little further on we ground to a halt, sitting in the baking sun by the side of a deserted sliproad, eating duck's heads and ants. The duck's heads were my name for a bag of cheap madelines, whose shape suggested their name. The ants were ants. We decided that they tasted like crunchy lemon juice.

Over several hours we were joined by more and more hitchikers, of many different nationalities. People got dropped here, but no-one left. In the end we all formed a line across the road trying to flag down any approaching vehicles. The cars just kept driving. Eventually a hippy bus pulled up, the temporary home of a bunch of men from Birmingham. The Brummy men on board said we could all get a lift, as long as we all contributed a little to the cost of fuel. They were heading in a loop back to a motorway and then north east into Germany. This was the opposite direction to the one we wanted, but we decided to go with fate.

The blokes on the bus had been travelling randomly all over Europe for several months. They had a stove on board and pots and pans. Everyone put some money in a hat and we had a meal together. They drove us back through Mulhouse in a fraction of the time we had taken in the opposite direction; and on, over the Rhine and back into Germany. They dropped us in Frieburg.

We decided to head back for the Ruhr to where we had been made most welcome. Slowly, but uneventfully we made our way north, back to Ziggy and Rosi's house. We arrived there at about eleven o'clock at night. Their lights were off, and we didn't want to disturb them, so we wandered to the edge of town, and just past the last street light, put up our tent.

We were awoken early the next morning by a barking dog and a man shouting at us. When I emerged from the tent I realised why he was angry. We had pitched our tent on a lawn at the end of his long garden. We quickly dismantled the tent and then ambled away. Near Rosi and Ziggy's we waited until we saw them come out of their house, and then walked past their car offering a nonchalant wave. They burst out laughing, and drove us into Düsseldorf.

We spent a few more days, again in a cloud of cannabis smoke, with our friends in the area. We played more music and recorded a cassette's worth, which we promised to release on NB when we returned home. Attributed to the Hornsey Düsseldorf Picnic Corporation, the title of the tape translated into English as *All this for the Price of Soup in the Daydream Shop.*

We invited any of our friends that wanted to make the journey to come and stay with us and then we set off towards home. We stayed a night again with Hans Hauser, and then caught the ferry and train home.

Igor was delighted to see us back. He was also glad that he was no longer responsible for Ad Hoc, with whom he had never successfully bonded. He had arranged all of our post on Nag's bed – there were a few letters each for Nag and me, and nearly seventy for NB Records.

The End

Back at home in early September we busied ourselves duplicating the Picnic Corporation tape and covers for it, and sent some over to Düsseldorf as a thankyou. It was good to escape from the cloud of dope smoke. We wondered about our German friends – we had been indulging ourselves whilst on holiday, but did they smoke all the time?

We were offered a gig at the School House. Nag and Mark thought it was short notice, but I encouraged them, and asked Giblet if he would play with us.

The next morning I awoke to find two letters pushed under my door, one an envelope addressed to Nag and me, and the other an envelope from Nag with a note on it saying read the other letter first. Usually I was the first up, but Nag had beaten me today and had already gone out. Igor was still asleep.

The first letter was from Mark. He said that he didn't want to play any more gigs with TDATW unless they were planned well in advance, so that we could rehearse and be our best. He didn't want to play the gig at the School House that evening. He reiterated what he had said before about wanting to take our time and not get drawn into the usual rock and roll cycle of gigging and recording. Sorry, he said, to muck us about, but he'd like to meet up and plan our future.

Nag's letter said that he was in agreement with Mark, he also didn't want to play these "fast" gigs – especially since we didn't even know who would be playing with us tonight. He went on to criticise me for seeming to enjoy a ragged cluttered sound, and my unwillingness to rehearse. He was unwilling to play another TDATW gig unless he knew beforehand exactly what we were going to play.

Nag went on to say that it seemed to him that TDATW seemed to mean little more to me than a little bit of fun, and that since he shared the same attitude as Mark that I should leave the band. He had the right to say this because he took the band much more seriously, and because it had been his money funding the band!

I was miserable and I was furious. His money! Some of what Nag had invested in NB had been paid back to him as wages earlier that summer, the rest was sitting in the bank. His words were just mean. Why did he think that this band meant less to me than to him? It was the main focus of my life! Igor was up, and was sympathetic to my woes. I went out and wandered aimlessly. I found myself walking past where we had taken photos of semi demolished buildings for the first single. They had gone and the land was cleared. It felt symbolic. I ruminated on my thoughts from before we went on holiday – how it might be a crisis point for Nag and I. In actuality we had gotten on well for most of the holiday. The crisis had come afterwards.

The next day Mark and Nag and I met up at Mike's café to discuss where we were at. Nag announced what he felt – that I should leave. Mark just said simply – Well, if Bendle's out of the band, that's the end of The Door And The Window! And then he dispelled any tension or hostility between us by adding - It's great, when a band splits up – it means that we are all free – free to do anything! Suddenly, rather than an end, we had the excitement and potential of new beginnings...

PART TWO

Watford

Early in 1981 Ronald Reagan was elected as president of the USA. A more dangerous equivalent of Thatcher was running the most powerful nation on earth. Anyone who bothered to think about the state of the world feared that we were one step closer to the likelihood of nuclear war. This was a shadow that we tried to ignore but of which we were quietly always aware.

In January I was offered a couple of weeks work by a temp agency working in a large kitchen for the borough of Islington, cooking breakfast for dustmen. For the first week my job title was "cooking assistant", but when someone else left, my title for the second week became "cook". The work was the same – fry tons of bacon and loads of eggs, toast loads of bread. It was mundane, unskilled work that anyone could do – but it got a useful label attached to my name on the temp agency records. Subsequent to this employment I got a call from the agency offering me a placement in a children's home – You are a cook, is that right Mr Bendle? - I hesitated for a moment but then said yes. I worked at one home for a few weeks and then got a placement in a second children's home in the same area in North Finchley.

One of the staff planned the menus for the week and presented them to me. Some of the food was pre-ordered from regular suppliers, some I had a budget to spend in local shops. I found a recipe book in the kitchen and would open it to the right pages and place it in one of the drawers, carefully following the instructions, and multiplying up the amounts. If any staff or residents entered the kitchen I would shove the drawer shut and hide the book until they left. I was successful enough in bluffing my abilities that the second care home quickly offered me a permanent contract which I accepted despite my utter fear of the word "permanent".

The establishment was a home for young people taken into care by the council. The children ranged in age from seven to sixteen. It was the best job I had had. I'd cycle in to start at ten, preparing lunch for the staff and any children who were at home. I'd buy any food that I needed to and prepare dinner for around sixteen kids, several staff and myself. After eating dinner I'd wash up all of the large saucepans and implements that I'd used and set off for home, leaving the rest of the washing up to the kids. From the very beginning I refused to buy white bread, and said that if I was the cook that they would have home-made wholemeal bread – so I would bake bread every day and, finding that it was popular, also made a couple of pints of yoghurt daily.

I found myself in a central position in the house. I wasn't part of the care team, but the staff needed to keep me informed about the children, so I was briefed both formally and informally about their backgrounds and needs. The kids, on the other hand knew I was "just the cook" and felt they could tell me things in confidence that I wouldn't tell the proper staff. So, as they drifted in from school to the kitchen to collect bits of fruit and small snacks, they would tell me about their day's mischief making. On school holidays I was entrusted to take groups of them out for walks or on trips to the swimming baths.

Two of the teenage boys – white racist Two Tone ska fans – were physically bigger than me and were sometimes threatening. A third friend of theirs was placed temporarily in the home, and one day when I entered the building the three of them grabbed me and pinned me to the floor. They seemed to just need to demonstrate their physical strength and after a while let me go. Mostly the environment felt safe and it was unusual to feel threatened by the boys. There was a cassette radio in the kitchen and I would bring in tapes of Talking Heads and The Teardrop Explodes, which the teenagers would eject to replace with tapes of The Specials and Madness. I would make them listen carefully to the words of some of the songs they liked, pointing out the contradictions with their political inclinations.

The most dangerous of the residents was one of the youngest. Some of the horrible past that he had endured would erupt in him every now and again, when a misplaced word might trigger his transformation from a loveable boy into an explosion of fists and kicking feet. He had broken ribs of more than one member of staff and would be regularly subject to physical restraint by the staff – being held down until his temper dissipated. He returned home one day from therapy at the Tavistock Centre and asked me what was for dinner. He didn't like the answer and let me know it by rapidly throwing loads of empty milk bottles (from a crate by the kitchen door) one after another at me. I allowed him to let off steam, ducking the bottles, then cleared up the mess. I didn't want to see him being restrained again.

There was a young woman, a few years older than me, employed at the home as a cleaner who confided in me about her past. She had been diagnosed as schizophrenic and had been locked up in a mental hospital in Greece where she had been travelling.

She attributed this experience to being doped unwittingly with LSD. I enjoyed our conversations and, wanting to understand more about mental illness, started to read the books of RD Laing.

At some point after the demise of The Door and The Window, Nag and Mark had formed a new band called The Reflections with Dennis Burns from Alternative TV and Karl Blake from The Lemon Kittens. Nag had abandoned his Wasp and taken to playing the bass. He and Mark shared both singing and songwriting, and Mark played guitar. Karl played magnificent falling apart but somehow keeping the beat drums. Dennis played bass when Nag was singing and also saxophone. I was both a friend and a fan and attended all of their gigs.

I started the year quietly, musically. I'd played a couple of gigs with Simon Pearce under the name of In Which We Talk, but that had fizzled out. I was writing songs, but not performing them, but had written a little comic called A Temporary Solution – my musings on the meaning of life sketched around the framework of my mornings cooking breakfast for dustmen. I'd printed it as a 16 page A5 booklet and had been giving them away to people. I'd posted one to a bloke called Nobby Nils whom I knew originally as half of a duo (with Paul Jamrozy, later a member of Test Department) who did a fanzine called The Geek. Nobby was writing poems and suggested that we make a joint "magazine" to give away for free. Between us we bought some clear A4 plastic sleeves and put together two little booklets of Nobby's; a little booklet by his friend Illy the Fish of writing based on the ideas of Wilhelm Reich; my Temporary Solution and a copy of the Mark Perry/Dennis Burns single. We made about 50 copies of this little package and took half each to give away to people who looked like they might read it. I'd carry a few with me and pass them to people on buses or on the tube, or I'd give them to people as I cycled to work.

Vicky's sister Michelle had arrived in London at the tail end of 1980 and almost immediately hooked up with Nag. Somehow, without any discussion, she moved into Ferrestone Road, sharing Nag's room with him. I loved her company and was happy to have her in the house, but it changed the dynamic of the three of us, and Igor was a little left out. Igor was still working at Better Badges, and both Nag and Michelle were doing temp jobs – and so we actually had a little money coming into the house.

On a Monday morning in February Michelle went into work, and when asked by her fellow office workers – what did you do at the weekend? responded – We shaved Bendle's head! I'm not sure where we got the idea from but it seemed like a good idea to explore what the shape of my head was without hair. I thought it might threaten my employment status at the kid's home, but it didn't. The boss there commented that it made me look like the sort of person who writes books in prison. Cycling to work with a women's scarf round my head to keep out the cold my androgynous looks attracted wolf whistles from heterosexual men. And this increased as I started to wear eyeliner. I'd never been anywhere near the Blitz club, but little bits of the New Romantics' dress sense were influencing me. Nag had for some time been buying clothes in the Covent Garden shop Flip. Flip mostly sold retro American clothes, but they were the outlet for suddenly popular gas jackets and gas trousers. Presumably originally made as protective military garments, these cotton garments had been over-dyed in bright colours that sort of cracked through the original grey or green. It was the first time I'd been attracted to a trendy item of clothing, and bought a pair of the baggy trousers.

Also in February Nag, Michelle and I wangled free entry to the first London show by New Order at Heaven and all three of us plus Igor went to see Bow Wow Wow play at the Rainbow. Inspired by Green's ideas about subverting popular culture, Igor especially was keen to see what Malcolm McLaren's new band were up to and what was this thing about pirates? The Rainbow had removed all the seats for the gig and set up fairground stalls and a helter skelter inside the venue. The whole evening felt like a great party and we just enjoyed whatever was offered to us – including the support act who were a big swing band, and the appearance of seemingly out of it New Romantic celebrity Boy George trying to sing with the headliners.

I had become friends with a boy called Nigel Jacklin. He had band called Alien Brains and it was by this name that Nag and I referred to Nigel. In the same way that the 49 Americans were Giblet and whoever he chose to record or to play with, Alien Brains were Nigel and whoever was temporarily on board, now and again including me. Before even being known for his own band he was slightly notorious as the boy who had arranged for Throbbing Gristle to play at Oundle (public) School whilst he was a student there.

Alien lived in a flat in Lancaster gate with two Italian girls called Gogo and Doriana. I would visit them in their posh neighbourhood and explore it with them – both physically and sonically. Alien had an expensive hi-fi system, which mostly he used to play industrial music, at very low volume. Part of this set up included a high-end cassette deck, into which we would plug a good microphone, and dangle it from his second floor window low enough to pick up and record the night time conversations of people passing by. We would also wander the local streets at night gazing into the residences and hotels just to marvel at the chandeliers!

One day in February I took a day off from work to play a gig with the Liberated

Sound Octet. Cy was doing a course at the London College of Furniture in Aldgate, and had arranged for us to play a free gig there for the students. We were Cy, Chris the drummer, another friend of Cy's also called Chris, Gogo and myself. We all dressed in chef's clothes – white tops and checked trousers and we aimed to play music mostly on items connected with food. We began with a theatrical game of cricket played with French batons of bread and bread rolls. Gradually we began chanting and playing percussion – saucepans, food containers and bottles. I had a big metal oil drum which was a percussion instrument in itself, and also a receptacle for the bottles which gradually got smashed. Getting hot I stripped down to my waist and high on cathartic chanting and drumming tipped out all of the broken glass from the drum and rolled around in it. My energy made me impervious to the glass. Meanwhile the students backed away from us in fear until Cy opened a big window. It was raining outside and Cy wanted to play the wet glass with a chunk of polystyrene, but the students feared that we wanted to throw the bar piano out of the window. The gig was stopped and we ground to a halt. I brushed the broken glass from my skin, bemused that I wasn't cut nor even scratched, and took a full two days to settle from my ecstatic adrenalin burst.

Early in the year I had whizzed off to Paris for a couple of days with two people I hardly knew. Barny Boatman, a maverick who liked inventing board games, whom I'd met through the Scritti Politti crowd, and Gina, an American who was working in Rough Trade. We had bumped into each other in a bar in Camden, and when Barny said – it's boring here – let's go to Paris – we did! He drove us to our homes to collect passports and off we went. Our journey was not straight forward due to strikes which meant no connection between rail and ferry services, but we travelled in style, Barny ordering us a champagne breakfast just before we hit Calais. When we finally got a train connection and made it to Paris we wandered all the tourist locations, fuelled with wine and coffee. I was immensely inspired by the Pompidou Centre and the whole trip was an excited blur.

Now in March I returned to Paris on a trip with Snotcher. It was a more sedate journey and whereas I was happy to blindly wander, he was keen to plan our days and to look for subcultural stuff. We took the metro to Babylon thinking the name hinted at something interesting, but were disappointed. We stayed in a cheap hotel in Montmartre - £10 for the two of us per night, but found it harder to find cheap food and beer. He was as delighted as me with the Pompidou. I enjoyed the first holiday with my brother for some years, and it was great to be on foreign soil together. Travelling back on the train to Calais we sat in the bar compartment of the train and got talking (in English) to a French couple. They said that we looked less like hippies than them, that we were less likely to be stopped by customs officials –

would we carry their drugs into the UK? We declined.

Back in London Nag began to plan a trip to Australia. Michelle only had a visa for 6 months stay. Nag said he would follow her back and spend 6 months in Melbourne. Michelle suggested that I come too. In order to save funds for the trip all three of us took on extra work. We all managed to get work as Census enumerators, working at evenings and weekends on top of our other jobs. We were given three adjacent areas to tackle, so were able to help each other out – dropping off forms, calling back to advise people re filling in information and to collect the forms. Michelle suggested that we go to the pub before setting out on our initial run of delivering the forms, so we all began the job somewhat tipsy.

Vicky's friend Debbie came to visit with her new boyfriend Chris. This tall gentle bloke from County Durham seemed great company to Nag and I (and became a long-term friend), but Igor freaked out when he found out that Chris was a policeman. We tried to reassure Igor – Chris had been in the audience when Chain of Dots played the Nashville and remembered the gig fondly.

Patrik Fitzgerald invited us to his flatmate's party – Nag, Michelle and I went. It was a weird do with just a few quiet people sitting around until a little group of skinheads turned up and began happily dancing. Each time one of them got near to Nag or me, they'd give us a little kick. At first we were scared, but they didn't feel like painful kicks... slowly it dawned on us that these were gay skinheads with an odd way of trying to pick blokes up. We were rescued by the guy that lived in the flat below. He took us down to his flat, littered with strange S & M equipment on the walls, where he played us some old 78's. On an old wind-up gramophone he played his collection of music. All of the songs were old jazz numbers whose subject matter was either sex or drugs. He offered drinks from his huge old American fridge, which seemed to be filled with nothing but dozens of cans of beer. He was a great host, furnishing us with lines of sulphate as well as amusing anecdotes and introducing me to a load of music which I had no idea had ever existed. Late that night we got a taxi home. When Nag and Michelle went to bed I realised that I was still 110% awake from the speed. I sat on my bed with a pile of paper writing first a new song and then rewriting others that I'd been working on into the early morning, and finally went to sleep excited that I had an album's worth of material.

We went to see The New Age Steppers play with Creation Rebel at North London Poly. The former were a reggae band featuring Ari up from the Slits singing. The gig didn't seem to get started. A couple of musicians strolled on stage and began to play, a third joined them, but one walked off... A bass player and a drummer played a rhythm. A man behind me in the audience tapped me on the shoulder and asked for a light. This turned out to be John Lydon, and my only communication with him was to reply that, sorry, no, I didn't. Bored of waiting for something to happen on stage I jumped up and starting singing, improvising words on the spot. It took several minutes for people from the venue to evict me, and I got a little round of applause for my efforts. Soon afterwards (at a small club) I also jumped up on stage to join in with a band called Pigbag – this time my efforts at collaboration were due more to exuberant enthusiasm. I sang a little bit of scat stuff and spent the rest of the gig dancing like mad to their fast funky drumming and their big sounding brass section.

I decided to take Giblet along to see Pigbag the next time I noticed a gig of theirs advertised. We turned up at the Tabernacle in Notting Hill, but somehow nothing was on. We wandered around to the Rough Trade shop to see if there were any ads in the window for any other gigs in the area. There we met a girl called Susi who was doing the same, and like us had come to the area to see Pigbag. There was no sign of any substitute entertainment so the three of us went to the pub together. We seemed to share similar enthusiasms and enjoyed each other's company. A man on the next table was reading a copy of Jane's Military Aircraft. He left the magazine on the table whilst he went to the toilet. Susi grabbed it and removed a number of pages. We made them into paper aircraft and sent them flying towards the man as he returned from the toilet and we exited from the pub. Infatuated with her from the moment of having met, I invited Susi to a party at my house that we'd planned to celebrate both my birthday and also Michelle's.

Meanwhile I planned the recording of my album's worth of material. Planned as a "solo" recording I invited a number of people to join me in sessions that I booked at The Street Level studio – Nag, Mark and Dennis; Giblet and Vicky. Michelle would play drums and Igor play keyboards. I also invited someone called Tony Clough who played guitar amongst other things and his friend Dave Morgan, who turned out to be a brilliant drummer who played wonderful Jaki Liebzeit style locked grooves. I'd hoped to get Grant to engineer the recording for me, but he was tied up with other projects, so I arranged for Kif Kif to do it. Due to my work commitments I had to arrange to do the recording in instalments rather than in one intense burst, and needed to make sure that I did the recording with Michelle before she went back to Australia. She had also been instrumental in introducing me to recordings of songs of Aboriginal Australians that were the inspiration for the sound of the first song that we recorded (called *Empty*).

Michelle and I had a huge party for our birthdays and as something of a send-off for her. Susi came and stayed the night in my bed. Quickly I found myself more intensely involved than in previous relationships, and I found Susi more inspiring than previous partners. A drop out from an art degree, she took me to galleries and introduced me to loads of visual art and to the ideas of Joseph Beuys. Susi also encouraged me to spend more time at the Film maker's co-op. I'd not attended many screenings there despite it being in the same building as the LMC. She was a fan of the abstract and avant-garde films of people like Stan Brakhage and Maya Deren. My feelings about these films were similar to those I had about LMC evenings – that there were occasional jewels amongst the dross.

Susi also introduced me to the music of Fela Kuti, played on a little stereo in her bedsit on the hill above Brixton. We decided to write a song together for inclusion with those I was recording. I had come up with the title *Optimism/Squirrel/Absurd* for the album. The song I wrote with Susi was called *Red Squirrel*. It included a line that I had stolen from one of Nag's Reflections songs: There's politics in every sausage. It took me a while to see the implications of this...

Around the time I was recording *Optimism/Squirrel/Absurd* Giblet had been recording an album with the 49 Americans. Neither Nag nor I were invited to participate – the band that had started off as a rabble was now recording an album of accomplished pop songs in an eclectic range of idioms and styles – Else's drumming was central, but most of the musicians were plinky plonk types from the LMC including Steve and David, Peter Cusack and Lol Coxhill. And Nag had recorded an album with The Reflections - who had signed a multi-album contract with an independent label called Cherry Red.

Giblet was going to issue the 49 Americans album on his own Choo Choo Train label, but I felt that the bubble had burst in terms of the hundreds of bands recording and releasing their own records also being able to sell them. When I finished the Optimism recordings I took them to Rough Trade with a view to getting them to release the album. They declined, saying they could see little progress from my TDATW material. I was upset and surprised since the music seemed completely different to me. I spoke to Mike Alway from Cherry Red who expressed interest but then prevaricated re making a decision about putting out my stuff. I decided to issue a cassette "pre-release". Somehow there was a market for albums on cassette. Alien released his stuff this way and people from the School House were involved in a cassette label called It's War Boys. Friends of Alien's ran a label called Snatch which had links with a new cassette label called Touch. Tony put out stuff on his label, Conventional Tapes.

I designed a cover and also a booklet of lyrics. Igor had left just Better Badges but had bought a share in an offset printer along with a bloke called Mark Schlossberg. Mark had found a workshop space, but the two of them needed some more cash input to get their new business off of the ground. I didn't know Mark, but trusted Igor's judgement and I offered to put in £100 for a third share of the press. They accepted and taught me how to use the machinery. So I printed my own cassette covers (on A4 paper) and the lyric booklet. I paid to get cassettes duplicated and made myself a stencil with the album title to spray-paint advertising for it. I caught tube trains early in the morning and daubed them with the three words, and undaunted by my previous conviction, sprayed the words onto walls in Hornsey. I felt too busy to keep up my employment in the children's home and left.

I decided that I had blown too much of my savings on the printer and on the recording of Optimism to afford a ticket to Australia, and blew another £100 on a professional Recording Walkman. The Walkman cassette players were still relatively new. The recording one seemed amazing. It had options on using the built in stereo microphones or external ones, had recording level and varispeed controls. I took to carrying it everywhere and recording everything. I visited Max Eastley with Giblet and recorded us opening his gate and walking up to his door. When we got inside we found that he had a similar recording from the other side of the door. He'd been recording the sound of a dripping tap, but had picked up our conversation on his path. I recorded the sound of his cat snoring.

I decided to form a band of some of the people from the Optimism recordings. I decided that my band should have an equal number of males and females, so the initial line up was Tony on guitar (and various other things), Dave on drums, Vicky on bass, Me singing and playing percussion, Tony's girlfriend Ashleigh on keyboards, and Susi playing whatever she felt able to. Tony, Dave and Ashleigh also played in the line-up of the next Liberated Sound Octet gig at Stanley buildings, along with Cy and Chris and myself.

For the LSO gig we collected loads of junk furniture and set up a layout like a bedsit – including a kitchen sink plumbed in with a hosepipe – in the garden at Stanley Buildings. The area we used faced out onto the road between King's X and St Pancras stations where we hoped that an audience would gather, although in the event most of our audience was composed of bemused prostitutes who worked that stretch of road. We used the furniture as percussion and gradually reduced it all to splinters. Some of the larger items got carried up to the roof, set on fire and lobbed from the top. So what if we had no audience? We purged ourselves of any bad energy and felt energised and happy at the end of it.

The Casual Labourers shifted through several line-ups. Susi had invited her actor friend Tim Roth to play trumpet with us for a couple of gigs, but then she herself left the band because she felt musically incompetent. Vicky drifted away at some point, and despite my intentions the band ended up as mostly male, with Dave, Tony and Ashleigh and myself being the only constant members.

Nag and I got a phone call – would TDATW play a gig in Watford? We had a chat about it. Actually, why not? We asked Mark and Dennis who both said yes, and we rehearsed a mix of old TDATW stuff and a few Reflections songs and a few of mine. After a gap of about a year The Door and The Window were playing again. Protag had moved to London and had a van in which he would drive us to Watford. Mark from the Automatons was around and came along too. Susi came and was roped in as a percussion player. Chris and Debbie came along for the ride.

The gig was in a community centre. There was a reasonable sized audience, but we were not sure they were keen to hear us – it seemed they were starved of bands and had just turned up to hear whoever was on. When we played we pointed out that we had copies of Detailed Twang to give away. They were enthusiastically retrieved from a pile on the stage – though we found several dumped in the toilet at the end of the gig. Half of the audience were drawn in and interested in what we were doing – many of whom gradually joined in on the bunch of junk percussion we had brought with us. The other half of the audience chatted away uninterested. Sod them! We were playing brilliantly – especially for a band that had split up a year ago!

The gig was a one off, but Nag and I felt that TDATW gigs were possible in the future.

Somehow, despite my going into business with Igor, relationships in our household had broken down. Nag and I were fed up with his lack of participation in keeping the place clean and his reluctance to do the washing up. He felt that it was wrong to be concerned about such things. Asked to wash up more frequently he said that we should buy more crockery! Take It were turning into a neo swing band – they sounded great, but we referred to their sound contemptuously as "Gigolo music". Nag was heading off to Australia in a matter of weeks and decided to move out. If he was going, then I was going too. And so we both moved out, found a temporary home for Ad Hoc, stored a few meagre possessions at Nag's Mum's house and became homeless...

Squeekybop Jugband

There's politics in every sausage...

I'd spent three weeks being homeless, sleeping on friend's settee's and floors, but by the time Nag left for Australia (driven to the airport by Protag, and waved off by the pair of us) I was living with Giblet and a man called Talent Scout in New Barnet. It was a great short-term rent-free arrangement with the landlord (who was Giblet's employer), and subsequently I moved into a small flat with Susi's friend Hetty – for a low rent in posh St. John's Wood.

Whilst sharing the house with Giblet my relationship with Susi dissolved into friendship rather than romance. I immediately hooked up with a woman called Pomme who I'd met though the Tufnell Park Mob. I had planned to visit Berlin ever since the TDATW gig there had fallen through, and had discussed the possibility of going there with Susi. Now Susi, Pomme and I set off for Berlin together and spent most of December 1981 living there in a large squat. There was conscription for young people in West Germany at the time, but this could be avoided if you were living in West Berlin. Presumably this was intended as a way of keeping a viable population in this little island of the West inside East Germany, but it functioned to produce a city full of anarchists. There were affluent parts of the city, but we were surprised to find many bombed out buildings left half standing since the end of the 2nd World War.

The three of us spent an intense few weeks trying to work out what our relationships with each other were. Susi and Pomme worked on a performance together exploring the ideas of borders – between countries, between that which is personal and that private, between people, all informed by the presence of the Berlin Wall. I taped as much as I could of our conversations on my Walkman cassette (and later transcribed them all), and all three of us constantly wrote in journals and notebooks. At first we shared a large room with one of our hosts, and then were given a room of our own in a huge building in Shonenberg.

There were dozens of squats used as large communal homes, many also accommodating cafés, bars, cinemas, arts and health centres. All of them bravely announcing their illegal presence with huge banners and murals. The people we stayed with were old long-haired hippies, plodding along at a slow pace whilst discussing armed revolution. We ate long breakfasts together of black bread and eggs (boiled in an electric kettle), with quark and slices of cold meat, endlessly discussing the politics of everything. I spoke no German, so sometimes was left out, or was translated to by my companions, but often our hosts spoke kindly to us in broken English. Marianne Faithful's song of that title – *Broken English* – was playing in bars across the city and became our theme tune. There were various subcultural groups in Berlin, but whereas in London they would be antagonistic towards each other, here they all seemed to feel part of a common movement.

Whilst Pomme and Susi wrote and rehearsed their show I met up with some young Germans and played and recorded a little music. We bumped into Gareth, who had been in the Pop Group, with his companions Springer and Sean Oliver from their new band Rip Rig and Panic. They put us on the guest list for a show in a large venue, and uninvited (but not rejected) I jumped up on stage and joined the band for the last half of their set.

We attended a large anti-NATO march which felt much more scary than marches in London, hemmed in by armed police with riot shields as we walked through a city where it seemed that every bank had a smashed window. At one point the police blocked the road, and I found myself at the front of a section of marchers facing the riot shields. Everyone automatically linked arms to face the police, me too, although my inclination was just to run away.

In a museum we saw a huge Indian swastika mosaic on the floor. I felt shocked seeing this ancient symbol in this particular city. All of our recent urgent discussions about politics suddenly seemed contextualised by a sense of timelessness and of contradictions.

By the time we left Berlin Pomme and I were definitely a couple, but Susi had decided that the only way to live her feminist principles was to explore a separatist lesbian way of life, and would soon move into a separatist feminist shared house. Pomme would find this a challenge to her own chosen heterosexuality – was she able to be a real feminist, but also be in a relationship with me? Over the coming months (and years) we discussed any and every aspect of our relationship, both keeping reflective analytical journals to which the other had open access. We tried to question every aspect of relating that would normally be taken for granted. Our love fizzed and popped – we had intense times together and then would part company, only to ping back together again.

On New Year's Eve Pomme and I met up with Susi and a few other friends to attend a reggae gig at a community centre in Brixton. Our little gang were the only white faces in a hall packed with friendly West Indians of all ages. As we danced I realised that in my urgent skanking dance I was moving at precisely twice the speed of those dancing around me. I breathed in the cannabis fumes and learned to move in a different rhythm.

Politics informed my life as we moved into 1982. With a shock I realised that nearly every book I had read had been written by a man, and decided that I would only read female authors for a year to try to balance things up. I'd already begun my feminist education by reading the heavy book of theory Gyn/Ecolgy by Mary Daly, and followed this up by reading Susan Griffin. I became a fan of the novels of Doris Lessing and of Marge Piercy.

Soon after moving in with Hetty I became friends with a boy called Mark. He was a tape operator at the famous Abbey Road studios. We began recording music, and found that we worked easily together. We'd record onto his four-track recorder at night, working with headphones so as not to disturb Hetty. I was still a crap musician but realised that although not great at playing live, I was good at building music layer by layer, using Mark's many effects boxes on our guitars. I was excited – producing what I took to be the best music I had been a part of. We played live together as a duo and Mark also played a couple of gigs with The Casual Labourers. Hetty was inspired by my musical friends and took up playing the bass.

Mark and I also began a project under the name of The Art Thieves. On tube trains there were adverts printed on thick cardboard running in series along the length of the carriages above head height. They were about 80cm by 20cm, and were slotted into a metal frame. We would go out with a rucksack and remove a number of adverts. Then we would process them. Carefully, working with a scalpel we would cut out pictures from colour magazines and add them into the adverts. Some of our completed collages were obvious political comments, some were just surreal modifications. Hetty was doing an art degree and had skills that we employed to help us. Most of our creations were subtle – you'd have to to look twice to notice all the starving emaciated faces looking through the window of the luxury residence, or the female head on a be-suited man's body. We would then return the adverts back onto tube trains. Usually just one per carriage, removing a fresh advert to replenish our supply. All of our altered adverts were signed with a little Art Thieves logo.

Bendle

Bendle & Mark at the Idiot Ballroom Photo by Hetty

In April the UK entered into a stupid war with Argentina over a claim to the Falklands/Malvinas islands. Whilst it was dragging on into May, Mark and I travelled to Barcelona. We stayed with Argentinian friends of people from The School House, and in the evenings battled out a friendly version of the war over games of dominoes. Upon setting off on the journey I had said that I wasn't sure how long I'd be gone and gave up my half of the tenancy on Hetty's flat. Mark was more clear that he wouldn't be away for long and moved his belongings in in my place. Mark travelled back directly from Spain, but I slowly hitched my way up through France, returning to find myself homeless once again in London. I pitched my tent in Hetty's back garden and lived there for several weeks, doing temp jobs until I had enough money for a deposit on a bedsit in Notting Hill. Pomme's tenancy expired and she lived with me in the tent for a couple of weeks, prior to her moving into a squat in Charing Cross with a bunch of people from New Zealand.

The Casual Labourers played a number of gigs, mostly in London and often with a band called The Work or with The Murphys, or both. I was constantly trying to analyse what it meant to be performing on a stage and we tried to break down the gap between audience and performers by taking lots of percussion instruments to gigs to hand out so that the audience could join in. I felt very disillusioned after a gig in Coventry and decided to stop the activity of the band. I was feeling very negative about the world generally having been attacked and knocked unconscious the night before the gig by a burglar who I happened to spot breaking into a property. In Coventry my face was still all bruised and swollen.

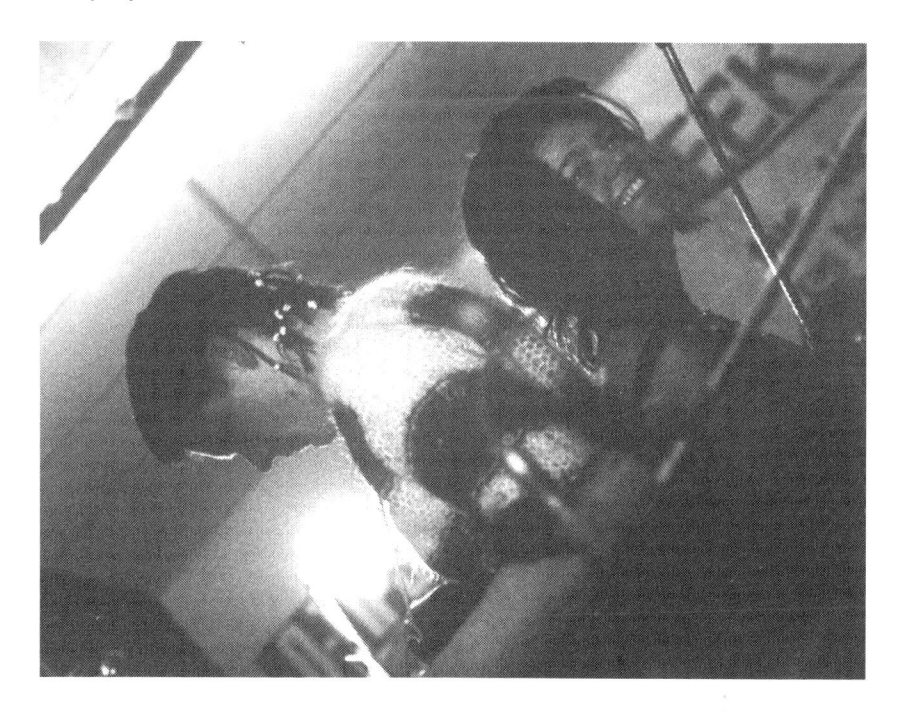

Bendle and Pomme in the Casual Labourers, Goldsmith's College. Picture by Hetty

In the summer I attended the first Big Green Gathering at Worthy Farm where that year the Glastonbury festival extended itself first into a women only camp and then the Green Gathering. The women's protest camp at Greenham Common (against the USAF cruise missiles located there) had been established in the autumn of '81, and their actions were a focus of discussions at the gathering. There were big debates where amazingly mostly just one person spoke at a time (in a marquee holding perhaps two hundred people). Should Greenham be a women only camp? There were some blokes who thought not, but the women's arguments triumphed. At the gathering I met Keith Motherson whose name I knew from the pages of Peace News. With his partner, feminist painter Monica Sjoo, he had co-authored a book propounding a mixture of anarchist and feminist viewpoints. He introduced me to men from the Men's Anti-sexist Movement, and back in London I attended the first national gathering of this group.

Mark attended the anti-sexist gathering which prompted a couple of forays into Soho together. We attached little notes reading "from Boys against Sexism" to tomatoes with elastic bands, and threw them at the men guarding the doors to sex shops. We escaped unscathed, but decided not to repeat this more than twice. We also very narrowly escaped arrest for our Art Thieves activity, jumping the barrier at a tube station and running off in different directions from a policeman.

By wangling a way of making telephone calls for free, Nag and I had been in regular contact whilst he was in Melbourne. Later in the summer he returned from Australia, moving in for a while with his parents. He had overstayed his visa, trying to extend his time with Michelle, but had had to leave. I moved from my bedsit to a shared house in Crouch End with two people I had met through the Anti-apartheid movement, but when one of them proved to be slightly bonkers I welcomed the opportunity of sharing a flat with Nag.

We sublet a one bedroom flat from Tim, an ex-boyfriend of Nag's sister, for a fixed term of 6 months. It was in a little block of private flats on Northwold Road in Clapton in East London. We were surrounded on all sides by a grim council estate. Our little block was seen as affluent and was a target for theft. We noted that any cars parked outside for more than a couple of days had their wheels stolen, and sometimes got torched. We flipped a coin and Nag got the bedroom. We partitioned off part of the front room with improvised curtains pinned to the ceiling to be my bedroom. We moved any of Tim's belongings that we didn't need into a tiny box room. When he came to see how we were doing he asked what had we done with the microwave. We explained that it was in the box room. Then how did we cook?! And why had we painted a picture onto the TV screen? Without discussing why, we subsequently referred to our landlord as The Green Blob.

The grimness of our immediate environment prompted me to wander further afield to explore Hackney Marshes and to take the local overground train to part of Epping Forest. Still within the boundaries of London, I delighted in the presence of water voles, nuthatches and treecreepers.

Nag had got a job working as a VDU operator for a company making tiles. I was signing on again, but we both did a little work for Nag's Dad. Michael had recently stopped running a stall on Ridley Road Market in Dalston that he'd had for years. Through this he had met some guys that ran a disco in Tottenham who offered him the food franchise there. Naive Michael liked these blokes, who treated him well, but they seemed like rather evil crooks to us. On Saturday nights Michael needed extra staff, and we helped cook burgers and chips in the horrible meat market dance hall. We later found that our misgivings about the owners were justified when some of them were arrested and jailed for the smuggling of South African gold into the country.

Speaking of South Africa – I was still involved with the Anti-apartheid movement. I spent a couple of nights camping on the pavement outside of South Africa House on Trafalgar Square where there was a permanent 24 hours a day protest, with a constantly changing group of protesters. I always felt a little on the edge of the group that I belonged to, never knowing the words to Nkosi Sikelel' iAfrika that inevitably got sung in large meetings. And the protest seemed a little earnest with a "university of the street" happening each evening. I had organised a benefit for AA earlier in the year with a line-up of The Promenaders[iii], The Work, The Casual Labourers and The Murphys. On the night The Promenaders suggested that they play first since they were acoustic and would sound too quiet if they played after the other bands. We had a quick discussion with the other bands and decided to play in the order we were listed on the poster. A few punters complained that they had missed the acts that they had turned up to see, but mostly the audience was happy. The evening ended with people dancing to the Murphys – on the crowded dancefloor and also on the tables!

People had heard that Nag was back and that we were sharing a flat together. The Door and the Window were invited to play a gig at the LMC. Nag and I had enrolled in a T'ai Chi class in Parliament Hill. It was awkward to travel there from Clapton, but the teacher was brilliant so it was worth the effort. Our gig at the LMC was on a T'ai chi evening, so we said that we would turn up after the class, missing the support group, but using their instruments.

Emerging from the T'ai Chi class we felt grounded, clear and meditative. We weren't sure if that was how we needed to be for a performance so we bought a can of Special Brew each and drank it on our way to Camden. Taking the stage, slightly inebriated, but still somewhat meditative, we thanked the audience for being there, and explained that TDATW had not played in London for ages because we had been on tour in Japan. We then proceeded to demonstrate our T'ai Chi moves before improvising some songs. We made use of the LMC piano and the drum kit, guitar and bass that were there. There was no PA and this was perhaps the most quiet, tentative performance that we had ever done together. We were psychically linked by way of the T'ai chi and the beer and made delicate, though discordant, music. The feedback afterwards from people in the audience suggested that we came across like two charming but bemused schoolboys wondering how we had ended up on stage. We were drawn to a man of about our age in the front row of the audience who had beamed throughout our performance. When we asked, he said his name was Ruskin. We invited him to dinner. He asked if he could bring his friend, who was with him. We took a look at his friend, and said that sorry, no – his friend had a beard, he was not welcome.

At home we cleaned the TV screen so that we could watch some of the launch of Channel 4, proclaimed to be a station with radical content. They screened a programme about animal rights called The Animals Film, narrated by Julie Christie, and soundtracked by Robert Wyatt. Nag declared at the end of the film that he was now a vegetarian, joining me in a change that I had made some months before. His sister had given us The Moosewood Cookbook of vegetarian recipes and we decided to work our way through it, learning new things. We made a list of about 50 people that we would like to invite to dinner, and did so, a few at a time. We split up couples, inviting people on a different night to their partners. We invited Bobo Phoenix to the first evening with three others and he said it was the nicest thing he'd done for ages. We decided to have him as a permanent guest and put him on the list for each week. When we got to the end of the list we invited people from the lonely hearts column in City Limits[iv]. We explained that we were not looking for romance, but that we would invite several of the people with the most interesting adverts on the same night.

The squat that Pomme was living in was evicted and she moved in with me for a while until she found a room in a shared house in Brixton.

TDATW were invited to play again at the LMC. We accepted, but this time decided to write some songs and practice them first. The Casual Labourers had played no gigs after Coventry, and The Reflections had split up in Nag's absence, despite the contract. So TDATW was for now our sole musical outlet. We borrowed a drum machine – suddenly quite cheap but sophisticated models were available – and I made us a selection of backing tapes using this. Our first song was called Jack Bishop Imitators inspired by our experience that:

> In the flat where we live
> Jack Bishop's the caretaker
> But he's not the real Jack
> He's just an imitator

and that Clapton was full of Jack Bishop Imitators!

We also played a gig where we'd gotten Snotcher on the bill with his mate Tony and they had come up to London especially. Snotcher had written a couple of long songs called Engineer parts one and two about his apprenticeship and work in the railway works in Swindon. Nag and I played as part of their band. The pair of them were completely disorganised and incredibly nervous. I was irritated with them and our performance was shambolic. Playing rather better than us that night were The Lowest Note on the Organ – friends of the Murphys, the Frank Chickens and the Murphys themselves. As the Murphys played Lance, one of their mates from the School House, inflated dozens of black bin liners with the outlet from a vacuum cleaner and gradually buried the band with them as they played. Despite this I left the gig in a bad mood on my own and ended up staying the night with friends in King's Cross.

Snotcher and Tony made their way back to Clapton before Nag and met our neighbour Brian. Brian was a composer who claimed his most well know piece was the "cookability" tune for a TV gas advert. He was incredibly friendly, and if we popped in to say hello, we would be drawn in by his welcome and a tumbler full of vodka, emerging hours later than planned. He told Snotcher that my floor was too uncomfortable and that he and Tony could stay with him. They took up the offer and Snotcher managed to reject Brian's sexual advances without even recognising what they were. Brian invited him back to stay whenever he wanted. Snotcher took up his offer, but disappointingly for our neighbour, turned up with his girlfriend Sue as well.

Nag packed in his job which meant that we were free to spend the whole day together before our next TDATW gig, at the Last Chance Centre in Hammersmith. We had roped in Chris Cornetto to play his trumpet and Protag to play as our drummer. Our written songs hadn't worked out very well at the LMC, so we'd decided to improvise this one. Walking around together all day talking gibberish to each other would get us in the zone: noting the bee shaped bit of detritus in our take away lunch we rhymed: hips, pips there was a honeybee in my chips, which would later surface in our "crapping" that evening. Crapping: a mixture of rapping and talking crap!

The other bands playing that evening were more straightforward acts – dismissed as boring by Nag and myself, and who probably didn't prepare the audience for us. So whilst we might not have gone down that well, we were pleased with our own performance. Except for Protag. Uncomfortable behind the drumkit he tapped out boring 4/4 rhythms until we evicted him. We'd recently seen the film Wise Blood and reused a line from the movie – "anyone who has a good car doesn't need to be justified". This over several repetitions evolved into "anyone who has a good car doesn't need to play in 4/4 time", which we repeated until we spontaneously both shouted : Sack the drummer! And ushered Protag off of the stage, continuing with Chris now playing the hall piano. We continued with a song about giving increasing amounts of money to tramps. When we clicked in with each other we could make up words easily and endlessly.

In December we decided that we liked the idea of running a cabaret club. We made a list of all the people that we might want to put on, our list headed with Syd Barrett and Vivian Stanshall. Ivor Cutler and Kevin Coyne were also near the top of our list. We went to visit some venues and settled on The Pindar of Wakefield near King's Cross, arranging to hire their back room on Monday nights starting in January. We flicked through a dictionary and threw together a couple of words to name our club: The Sprouts Conspiracy. Having got a venue and a name we decided to start booking acts. We decided that we hated the usual hierarchical payment structure and that each night we would have three acts and that each act would be paid the same fee: £50. Trying to access musicians we tried phoning record companies and then agents. We got laughed at and dismissed with our offer of £50. We decided that we knew enough people and that we could manage to get hold of artists' personal numbers – surely we could charm them? I found out a number for Kevin Coyne and phoned him. Why, he asked, would he want to play in a little venue in London for £50 when the next week he would be playing a big hall in Amsterdam for £1000? I said because we were the people who had heckled him at a gig a while back. He remembered the interchange, and said yes. We phoned Ted Milton from the band Blurt. We said that we had heard that as well as being a bonkers saxophonist that he also did weird puppet shows – would he do one for us? No, but he would read his poems if we billed him as "The Great Poet Milton". Deal.

Other people proved less easy – Syd Barrett was unobtainable. My conversation with Ivor Cutler went:

Hello – is that Ivor?
Do I know you?
Well, uh, no, but we have met–
Then kindly call me Mr Cutler.
Ok! Mr Cutler would you be interested in...

But he wasn't. We didn't get Vivian Stanshall's number and heard that he was having problems with alcohol, so we abandoned him. We looked in City Limits and chose a couple of performers simply because we thought their photos looked good: Gladys "Glitter" McGee, a pensioner from the East End who performed her own poems (wearing a glittery suit), and another poet, Benjamin Zephaniah who had a nice smile. We'd always liked the voice of the person who sang *Lose This Skin* on The Clash album *Sandanista* – Tymon Dogg, debating if the singer was a man or a woman. It transpired that he was a man, and yes he would play, with his drummer friend Richard Dudanski – who we were excited about because of his history with Public Image and the Raincoats. By choice or by chance we came up with a series of eclectic and brilliantly entertaining billings of poetry and music, film and comedy.

We wrote silly letters with our listings to City Limits and Time Out, managing to get reasonable sized bits of blurb printed in the magazines, often with photos. Chris Cornetto got his Dad to photocopy fliers for us at his workplace for free. The club was a great success. We lit the tables with candles and played music in between acts quietly so that people could chat without shouting. We failed, however, to keep the Sprouts Conspiracy running long term because we ran out of people that we could talk into playing for our low fees.

We decided to put ourselves onto the bill as TDATW on the same night as headliners sound poets Bob Cobbing and Clive Fencott. We planned that Nag and I would sing mostly improvised songs, with a band composed of Dave and Tony from the Casual Labourers, Chris Cornetto, and a couple of friends of Chris playing horns.

The week before the TDATW gig we suddenly got the idea that we could record an album. The Street Level studio had moved out of its subterranean hole, but had been set up in a truck as a mobile studio. Protag had gotten involved in its maintenance and running – we phoned him – could we come and record an album – now?

He told us not to be so bloody stupid. Ok, we said, what about late tomorrow night? He agreed, so we followed that phone call with others to the band – meet at Protag's rehearsal basement off of Latimer Road, at midnight tomorrow.

For this recording, we decided, TDATW would be a Squeekybop Jugband. To instil the right atmosphere we made the band sit silently on the floor, in candlelight, and we made them listen to the Syd Barrett song *Jugband Blues* (from the 2nd Pink Floyd album), three times over. Then we could begin. Nag and I played several instruments during the night, but mostly just sang. Either together or alternating we made up stories and songs. These tended to be surreal hyperbolic descriptions of our life in Clapton. Having sung about being the worst band on our first single, we now made a list of all the bands we considered ourselves better than. Nag made up a great song about refusing to pay The Green Blob any more rent, intoning "the cheque bounces" in such a way that I could imagine it physically bouncing down the road. The music worked, held together with Dave's brilliant drumming. The weakest points were perhaps my attempts to make politically correct modifications of some of Nag's outre warblings. We recorded straight onto two track tape, and allowed Protag to play around with live dub effects. We paid Protag by giving him Nag's bass guitar. Later in the week we got an angry call from Grant Showbiz saying that we owed the studio £39.

Our neighbour Brian was always inviting us into his house. Deciding we were skint and that we needed feeding up he took us out in his car for a meal to a Greek restaurant. Since we also needed educating, he then took us on a tour of East End gay bars and clubs, explaining the different types of clientèle catered to at each place. We took up his offer to use his two track recorder, and over several evenings edited down the music from the session with Protag in his front room. We subsequently released it as a TDATW cassette album titled Squeekybop Jugband

Living with Nag helped me ease off a little from my earnest political analysis of any and everything, and to relax into spontaneous nonsense although I continued to take part in demonstrations and protests. My Nan (my Mum's Mum) died that spring, and after the funeral in Swindon I went out with Snotcher and painted pro-Greenham Peace Camp graffiti. CND had gotten more interesting in its response to the ongoing threat of nuclear war, and at Easter 1983 organised a big march. This aimed to link the ordinance factory at Burghfield to the camp at Greenham fourteen miles away via the weapons research unit at Aldermaston in the middle.

I joined the blockade of Burghfield the day before the march, travelling on my own, but meeting up with people I knew. We sang songs and danced around the police and at one point a group of about fifty of us encircled a group of them whilst all sitting on each other's laps. We had a little ragged camp away from the protest area, and I slept there in a rat infested barn. This was my first of what would turn out to be many nights spent in peace camps and blockades outside of USAF bases over the next two years.

Dogs

Half an hour before a performance in the Vulcan, and we can't get it right. Tom is repeatedly intoning – Eat your Greens – in a deep E - and Nag and I are trying to add our lines – Or your teeth will rot... Or your skin will sag... But Ruskin, who is rapidly picking away at an acoustic guitar in some sort of African 6/8 rhythm, is insisting that we get it pitch perfect. How the hell did he get to boss us around? We'd only drafted him in at the last minute because, like Tom, he happened to have called in.

The Vulcan: one of the numerous pubs along the road around the edge of The Isle of Dogs. We'd performed there on the first weekend after we moved into a council "Hard to Let" GLC flat, subsequent to moving out of Clapton. Most of the pubs had musicians performing in them at weekends. On Fridays and Saturdays in the Vulcan the act was a duo called Spear and Jackson, on keyboards and drums. The keyboard player would sing, but for part of the evening they were open to floor singers. Nag and I had jumped up and improvised a song called *Woof Woof in the Isle of Dogs*. Every time we went back the locals would ask us to repeat it, but we had to admit that we couldn't recall the words. Hassled to make a re-appearance and wary of taking the stage at an uninspired moment, we wrote some words to sing with the in-house duo.

Subsequently we responded to invitations from Ron, the landlord, to do a couple of performances there as TDATW on quiet midweek evenings. The first gig involved a prop: a large map of the area that we had drawn, which included signs "to the Mean Time" across the river in Greenwich. We sang songs about local things – the cafe, the ever on-going roadworks, the recently opened supermarket, and were surprisingly warmly received by the locals.

When we moved in Dogs was mostly desolate – council estates dotted around the periphery, empty warehouses and docks in the middle. Although desolate it was a much more friendly place to live than Clapton and the docks were our swimming pools, the abandoned contents of warehouses sources for free furniture. We could wander through the wasteland (across the road from our estate) that we dubbed

Reality Park, and climb down ladders onto the shore of the Thames. We worked on a huge production called The Raising of The Titanic in Limehouse Basin with the theatre company Welfare State, and in doing so met loads of East End musicians and artists and dancers. We had an official council tenancy, but we acted as unofficial estate agents, helping friends squat the empty flats on our estate. Ruskin had become our neighbour this way. Cy and his partner Claudia had managed to get a legal tenancy in a neighbouring block.

Nag and I did various temporary jobs – both of us working in a sweatshop packing videos and acting as ushers for events in the Barbican Centre, me dispatch riding on my bike – whilst we played in various bands. Nag was exploring pop music by playing bass with The Ultraviolets and The Clams, whilst I was mostly performing solo. I was working with backing tapes and playing an old cronky organ and a clarinet – and getting lessons on the latter in a class across the Thames in Goldsmiths College. Every now and again the idea of TDATW would rise up and swallow us. Sylvia Hallet invited us in the autumn of '83 to play at a festival of "self-made instruments" at the LMC. Despite our ambivalence about improvised music, we continued to be involved in the London Musicians Collective. It was a good space to try out my solo performances and we'd become friends with Sylvia and her fellow members of British Summertime Ends – Stuart Jones and Clive Bell.

For the home-made instruments gig Nag and I bought cheap second hand furniture from a junk shop and modified it into instruments. A table became a large tongue drum, a front room cabinet got modified with the addition of machine heads and guitar strings, and its top also became a tongue drum. We incorporated a bunch of fire alarm bells (that I had retrieved from empty warehouses) and other percussion onto a large wooden frame. We made up simple songs to sing along with our clunky new instruments, and then tried to auction the instruments at the end of the gig because they took up too much room in our flat.

Soon after this we played a gig at the plinky plonk improv club The Clinker and disappointed the organisers by singing songs about things like feeding the cats, accompanying each other with rudimentary playing of flutes and a melodica. We'd written and learned a new set of songs in the couple of days leading up to the gig, scrawling the last one on the bus as we made our way to the venue.

Subsequently the time between TDATW performances got longer. Over the years Nag and I had attended lots of free gigs in the Meanwhile Gardens in West London, but we had never played there until we did a short TDATW set in 1984 with Tony and Dave and with Hetty playing bass. We had rehearsed songs but we both took liberties with the lyrics at the gig. Spotting the singer in the audience, and paraphrasing one of his lyrics, Nag started singing about plunging a six inch golden blade into the head of Nick Cave.

In 1985 I moved away from London and away from music, but we still managed a TDATW gig in 1986 again with Tony and Hetty. We were reviewed as sounding like The Incredible String Band, whom at the time I knew very little about – but was flattered when I listened to their great albums[v].

The next year we played our last gig before a long (and still ongoing) hiatus. Nag had organised another Jazz Punk Bonanza, and put us on the bill. Again we played with Tony and Hetty and also with a viola player called Eddhu Nan. Nag and I had originally met Eddhu playing in a line-up of the Scratch Orchestra playing Cornelius Cardew's The Great Learning. Eddhu was a Guildhall trained classical musician and composer, but he was comfortable playing our neo-folk/avante-punk music. We shared the bill with people also most well known from previous musical work: And the Native Hipsters – famed for their one hit wonder There Goes Concord Again, now playing brilliant sing-along chorus jazz punk; and Dom and Cass previously from Furious Pig. Dom and Cass were friends of Ruskin's, and we'd met them through him around the time they were recording an album of furious but virtuoso percussion based music under the name of Het. They sounded like nobody apart from maybe Harry Partch.

Since that time we have been having a protracted hiatus between bouts of TDATW activity. The 49 Americans played (surprisingly brilliant) gigs in 2013 – with both Nag and I in the line-up. This was after a gap of 30 years – the first gig was publicised as a reformation, but like TDATW we had never really split up in the first place.

Afterword

In 2017 TDATW released their first music for many years. The *Singing on the Roof* ep is available along with *Doctor Egg ~ Live Recordings 83 -87* on Bendle's Bandcamp page.

Detailed Twang has had CD, digital and vinyl re-releases via Overground Records.

All of the 49 Americans recordings have had several re-releases in CD and digital form.

Endnotes

i   Returned many years later by Igor to Joe Strummer!
ii   Named after a line from the Wire song Indirect Enquiries from the album 154
iii   Loxhawn Rondeaux (Lol Coxhill), soprano saxophone, vocals; Stuart Barfoot (Steve Beresford), euphonium, vocals; Steve Topp (David Toop), one string violin; Mike Simple (Max Eastley), one string violin; Derek Nyte (Terry Day), cello, percussion; André (Peter Cusack), guitar; Paulo 'sticks' Birrelli (Paul Burwell), drums.
iv   City Limits was a London listings magazine set up in competition to Time Out by staff who left the latter after it abandoned its co-operative principles.
v   The Hangman's Beautiful Daughter and The Big Huge.

Printed in Great Britain
by Amazon